Democracy and the Public Service

Democracy
and the Public Service

SECOND EDITION

FREDERICK C. MOSHER
University of Virginia

New York   Oxford
OXFORD UNIVERSITY PRESS

Library of Congress Cataloging in Publication Data
Mosher, Frederick C.
Democracy and the public service.
(Public administration and democracy)
Includes index.
1. Civil service—United States.
I. Title.   II. Series.
JK691.M65   1982   353.006   81-11089

ISBN-13 978-0-19-503018-1

To the memory of my father
WILLIAM E. MOSHER
and my colleague
ROSCOE C. MARTIN
both of whom devoted much of
their thought and their life work to
democracy and the public service

Preface to the Second Edition

During the early 1960s, Professor Roscoe C. Martin of the Maxwell School at Syracuse, supported by the Dean of that School, Stephen K. Bailey, invited me to join him in teaching the introductory course of Maxwell's year-long master's program in public administration. My lectures for that course would be edited by Martin and published in a new series by the Oxford University Press on Public Administration and Democracy, which was in fact the title of the course. The original edition of this book, the first in the series, published in 1968, was a revised version of those lectures given at Syracuse. A large share of whatever credit is due the book should go to my dear friend, Roscoe Martin, for I doubt that without his initiative and encouragement it would ever have been written.

This is the first book I have undertaken to revise, and I have discovered, as I am sure many others have before me, that a revision presents some hazards and problems that are different from an initial writing. After nearly fifteen years, as in this case, of a rapidly moving government in a fast changing society, it is inevitable that not only will facts and data change but so will ideas, perspectives, and emphases. Were I to have started afresh, in 1981, this book would certainly have been different from the 1968 version or from that

1968 version simply revised. But I was encouraged to believe that the basic themes and approaches of the older version have continuing value and interest by the fact that it is still sold and used about as much as it ever was. This has contributed to my confidence that most of those themes remain significant, even though some of their facets and manifestations have changed.

Those who are familiar with the first edition will find here a few significant changes: greater emphasis upon collective bargaining, particularly among professional employees; brief discussions of the impact of the Vietnam War, Watergate, and the Carter personnel reforms, especially the Senior Executive Service; greater recognition of the continuing and ever growing significance of the management influence on the administration of personnel, expressed in part by the addition of a new chapter 4; more attention (though still not in proportion to its importance) to equal employment opportunity and affirmative action. This edition includes little on what has been termed "new public administration" and "organization development", movements which were getting underway when the original edition of this volume was written and which found a considerable following in the late sixties and the seventies—in the wake of disturbances about civil rights and Vietnam. Adequate treatment would have required a great many more pages than this book could accommodate. Furthermore, other authors better qualified than this one have discussed these subjects in a great many other works.

Had I been a more prescient soothsayer in the mid 1960s, I might have foretold the strains that American democracy would undergo in the years following: the growing disillusionment in government generally; the fractionation of leadership in the Congress; the weakening of the political parties (especially the Democratic Party); the multiplication of interest groups, including those with narrow or single objectives; and the growing difficulty of achieving political compromises, let alone consensus. All of these would have their impacts on the public bureaucracies, themselves increasingly fragmented by specialisms and professionalisms tied to a greater or lesser extent with interest groups in the private sector, with committees and blocs in the legislatures, and with parallel professions in or outside of other levels of government. A perfect democracy is no more possible in the political sector than a perfect market economy is in the economic sector. But our efforts to attain and maintain a workable democracy have become more and more difficult.[1]

Some of the changes in the responsibilities of American governments have profoundly affected the nature and problems of the public services. Contrary to widespread popular impressions, changes in kind and in scope have been far more extensive than changes in dimensions. It is true that for many years after the Korean War state and local governments together were the fastest growing employers in the country; but that trend was to some extent counterbalanced by the federal government whose employment grew hardly at all in relation to the population except for a bump upward during the Vietnam War. Even state and local employment has leveled off and very probably will gradually decline in the future. Dollar expenditures have of course grown at all levels of government, but a large part of this increase has been a consequence of inflation and of increased population; the proportion of total governmental expenditures at all levels to gross national product grew from about one-quarter in the mid-1950s to about one-third in the late 1970s. The proportion has been quite stable for the last decade.

The more dramatic shifts have been in the ways that government money is spent and the kinds of things that public employees do. In the first place, a very large share of governmental money goes out in cash payments to citizens for social security, welfare, unemployment benefits, pensions of various kinds, medicare and medicaid, and many other such programs. Of all federal dollars, these comprise more than two-fifths. For these kinds of tasks, public employees do not make things or provide direct services. Rather, they dispense funds. They must see that those funds go to the right people at the right times in the correct amounts and, in some cases, are spent for the proper purposes. Such tasks involve check delivering, accounting, auditing, investigating, sometimes prosecuting. They also involve appraisal of the effects of the programs, and the making or proposing of changes in policy and regulation.

A second large category of federal financial transactions are in the form of cash grants from federal to state and local and from state to local. Grant programs have grown enormously in number and variety as well as in dollar amounts over the past fifteen to twenty years. There are now said to be about 500 different grant programs from the federal government alone, and grants amount to a little under one-sixth of federal expenditures and about one-third of state expenditures. The administration of these programs is a subtly difficult operation for it involves the joining of purposes of different jurisdictions whose objectives, perspectives, powers, and politics are often far different, the continuing contest between generalist and specialist views at every level, questions of political compromises and accountability, and many other sources of contention. But for my purposes, the dominant factor is that the officials in the granting governments— mainly federal and state—are not doing very much beyond planning, conferring and negotiating, regulating, overseeing, evaluating, and auditing the work of other governments. They are not themselves performing the governmental functions.

The third large category of public expenditures consists of those programs for which governments pay for goods and services and produce outputs themselves. At one time, this category constituted the great bulk of public expenditures. But the proportion of government outlays that goes for the purchase of goods and services—teaching of children and young adults, building of roads and dams and nuclear reactors, provision of police and fire protection, and assuring an adequate national defense—has declined steadily over the last twenty years. Now it comprises only about one-third of federal expenditures, three-fifths of all public expenditures. But the data on purchases of goods and services are also deceptive since a large proportion of these payments are actually made to institutions and people outside the government on contracts and subsidies of one or another of a million kinds. Reliable figures are not available, but it seems likely that nearly half of the payments for the accomplishment of government programs are made to private businesses and other profit institutions, universities and other nonprofit institutions, international agencies, foreign governments, and consultants and other individuals and firms. Indeed, governments hire others to plan for them, to make and change their policies, and to manage their programs.

Some of the broad implications of these developments in the middle decades of the twentieth century have been suggested elsewhere[2] and will certainly be discussed in much greater depth in the future. For present purposes, I would emphasize the growing interdependence of governments with their clients and their controllers, the American people. It is hard any more to distinguish what is private from what is public; what is national from what is international; what is federal from what is state or local; what is executive from what is legislative and what is judicial. I think it is not, as President Reagan suggests, a question of "getting government off our backs"; or, as some public officials might say if they dared, a question of "getting the people off our backs." We are meshed, interdependent, mutually intrusive. "We have found the government and it is us."

The problem of making government behave in the best interests of its members—that is, we the people—is the problem of democracy. A major part of that problem is the work and the decisions of those who perform as our agents—the public service. The developments of recent years have, I think, made the jobs of the public servants far more difficult and far more significant because of the interdependencies mentioned above. The issues raised in succeeding chapters of this work, particularly 1, 5, and 8, seem to me more than ever pertinent and complex.

But they are challenging, not impossible nor even discouraging, and I devoutly hope that the focus in this book upon problems may not add to the dislike and disparagement of government and those who work for it which now seem so virulent among the United States population. From the beginning of this country, it has been common to view the workings of government critically and suspiciously; to emphasize its weaknesses and failures rather than its strengths. Such perceptions were certainly explicable in the light of experiences in earlier centuries, and they probably have on the whole been healthy in their encouragement of honest and better performance. But the increasingly bitter and rancorous attacks upon the "bureaucracy" and the "bureaucrats" in recent years have been neither deserved nor constructive. It now seems that few aspiring political executives think they can run and be elected unless part of their campaigns consists of invectives against those appointive public servants upon whom they will be—and in some cases have been— dependent in carrying out their responsibilities if elected or reelected. This is a formula for distrust, breakdowns in communications, and low morale. And such attacks when directed against career employees are also a self-fulfilling prophecy. For not very many of the best people in the public services are likely to want to stay there when they are paid far below their peers in the private sector and are the butt of repeated charges of incompetence, dishonesty, and laziness by their neighbors, the media, and indeed their own bosses. Nor are potentially excellent candidates likely to be enticed into such a career when they have other choices.

In my opinion, the deprecations of the public services are

very largely undeserved—at least so far. There are weak spots, as there are in other areas and among other employers. But a substantial number of top political appointees in public offices, after long experience in the private sector, have compared their career public service colleagues favorably with those with whom they had worked earlier in the private sector. Employees of governments in the United States are the leading experts, not only in this country but in the world in a large number of specialized fields, from epidemiology to nuclear physics, from criminology to animal husbandry, from silviculture to oceanography. A large share of both social and physical inventions were made by public employees—and even more were financed by public money, usually on the initiative and with the guidance of public officials. We should take some pride that the first person in the history of mankind to set foot on the moon was an employee of the United States civil service.

It is probable that professors who write books and articles owe their greatest debts to their students—for ideas, insights, questions, doubts, different perspectives. Perhaps most of all because the students make the prospective authors think, doubt, organize, and verify or revise. I acknowledge with gratitude the help I have so received from several hundred students, mostly at the graduate level, over the last three decades at Syracuse, California (Berkeley), Virginia, and even or perhaps especially, the University of Bologna. I owe particular acknowledgement to Keith Axtell, my graduate assistant at Berkeley, who contributed some invaluable research to the first edition of this volume; and to Max O. Stephenson, Jr., my current research assistant, whose knowledge, curiosity, ideas, wisdom, criticisms, and—yes—solicitude have seen me through many of the shoals of this revision. I am also appreciative of another graduate student at Virginia, Charles Greenawalt, whose special studies on collective bargaining were of great help to the revision of chapter 7.

Over the years since the first edition was published, I have
received innumerable comments and criticisms on various of
its parts, of many of which I have sought to take account in
this revision. It would be impossible to list all those to whom
I am indebted. I am particularly grateful to four persons who
were asked to read the entire book again and criticize it both
in general and in particular before the revision was begun.
They are: Randy H. Hamilton, Golden Gate University;
Rosslyn S. Kleeman, U.S. General Accounting Office; George
S. Maharay, National Academy of Public Administration;
Gary J. Miller, Michigan State University.

Most of the drafts and manuscript of this revision were
typed by Cynthia Miller who combines with her skill, care,
and perfectionism at the typewriter, a nice sense of humor
and a justifiable degree of contempt for the author's typed
drafts and penmanship. The remainder was typed by Jean
Stewart who is also an excellent typist and who very probably
shares the same contempt.

The National Academy of Public Administration helped
by making me a member of its panel to review the implementation and effectiveness of President Carter's personnel
reforms; my sessions with the members of the panel and with
its outside witnesses were very informative. Finally, I would
acknowledge the facilities and support of the White Burkett
Miller Center of Public Affairs at the University of Virginia.

Charlottesville   F.C.M.
November 1981

Notes

1. For my ideas about a "workable democracy" I am indebted to Emmette S.
   Redford, *Democracy in the Administrative State* (New York: Oxford University Press, 1969), pp. 197 ff.
2. My own brief discussion of this enormous topic, "The Changing Responsibilities and Tactics of the Federal Government", appeared in the *Public
   Administration Review* November/December 1980, pp. 541–548.

Contents

Democracy and the Public Service

1

The Issues

This book undertakes no very exquisite or precise definition of democracy. Nor does it aspire to comprehend all the facets of democracy: majorities and their powers; minorities and their protections; nominations and elections; political representation; the immunities of citizens; or even administration, viewed as a powerful and anonymous entity in its relations with individual citizens. My focus here is upon the public service, in its relation to democracy both as an idea and as a way of governance. For this purpose it seems unnecessary to dwell upon disputable definitions of "polyarchy" or "consensual elite" or similar intellectual constructs. My premises are relatively clear and limited; that:

1. governmental decisions and behavior have tremendous influence upon the nature and development of our society, our economy, and our policy;
2. the great bulk of decisions and actions taken by governments are determined or heavily influenced by administrative officials, most of whom are appointed, not elected;
3. the kinds of decisions and actions these officials take depend upon their capabilities, their orientations, and their values; and
4. these attributes depend heavily upon their backgrounds, their training and education, and their current associations.

Perhaps the most concise, simplest, most widely accepted definitions of democracy were those implicit in the Gettysburg Address of Abraham Lincoln. Our nation was one "conceived in liberty and dedicated to the proposition that all men are created equal." And our Civil War was to ensure the survival of government "of the people, by the people, for the people." Clearly the one phrase of the triad which is distinctive for democracy is the second one, "by the people." The first would apply to government of any stripe, and the third to any of paternalistic flavor. But what does "by the people" mean? By *all* the people? If not, by which people? The early, hopeful answer was the former—*all the people*, deciding matters through discussion and debate and vote as exemplified by the Greek city-state and the New England town meeting.[1] Even this elementary pattern could not by itself be fully effective in the community because meetings could not be assembled on the hour every day to handle the continuing problems of government. So was devised the method, once removed from the people, of governance by individuals elected by the people, answerable to them and removable by them—i.e., representatives. Preferably, such officers would serve short terms within narrowly circumscribed zones of discretion and would be forbidden to serve more than one or two terms in office. Although we commonly associate the elected representative officer with legislatures and chief executives, the basic concept has applied widely in this country to administrative and judicial officers as well.

Reliance upon popularly elected representatives is one step removed from direct participative democracy. A second step occurs when officers so chosen select and delegate powers to other officers, appointed and removable by them. As the dimensions of the administrative tasks of government grew, these came greatly to outnumber the elective officers; and for

1. Though in neither case was participation open to anywhere near *all* the people.

a period in U.S. history, a substantial part of the public service were politically appointive and removable officers and employees. A third step away from direct democracy is taken with the designation of personnel who are neither elected nor politically appointive and removable, but rather are chosen on bases of stated criteria—social class or caste, family, wealth, general competence, specialization in given tasks and skills, etc. It is now of course clear that in every developed country in the world the vast majority of public officers and employees are in this category; that many of them command specialized knowledges and skills which give them unique competence in some field—competence that neither the general public nor its elected or appointed political officers possess. It is also obvious that they influence—or make—decisions of great significance, though within an environment of constraints, controls, and pressures, which itself varies widely from one jurisdiction to another, from one field or subject to another, and from one time to another.

The accretion of specialization and of technological and social complexity seems to be an irreversible trend, one that leads to increasing dependence upon the protected, appointive public service, thrice removed from direct democracy. Herein lies the central and underlying problem to which I address myself: How can a public service so constituted be made to operate in a manner compatible with democracy? How can we be assured that a highly differentiated body of public employees will act in the interests of all the people, will be an instrument of all the people? My focus in the pages that follow is upon the appointive administrative services, those sectors that are twice and thrice removed from direct democracy. My primary concern is with our experience, our practices, and our directions in the United States; but I include some references to other countries for purposes of contrast and comparison.

In this chapter, I should like to state some of the principal themes and sub-issues which have underlain the basic problem as it has evolved in American thinking. My purpose is to define and to establish a terminology. Most of the topics suggested here are treated later on in various connections. They include: policy-politics and administration; responsibility; representation and representativeness; mobility; participation; and the rights of public servants.

Policy-Politics and Administration

The concept that policy should be determined by politically responsible officials, institutionally separated from the execution of policy—i.e., administration—and the arguments attendant upon it are relatively recent in political and intellectual history. One finds little reference to them in the writings of many of the great political thinkers, and this perhaps reflects the general lack of concern they felt about administration. In much of this writing, there seems to have been an implicit assumption that administration is the obedient and willing pawn of whoever controls it; the primary issue then is the locus and the effectiveness of such control. The separation of policy from administration has been equated with the separation of the legislative from the executive power, but the division in both theory and practice has been a very rough one. In our own Constitutional debates and early political history, it was hardly contemplated that the executive would be or should be powerless on matters of national policy, and in fact certain specific powers with respect to policy were granted to the executive in the Constitution itself.

The emergence of the doctrine of institutional dichotomy between policy and administration seems both logically and historically to have followed two basic developments. First was the rise of representative democracy in the Western countries during the eighteenth and nineteenth centuries, expressed primarily through legislative bodies and the emergence of political parties. One of the chief objects of contest became the control of administration—of its positions, its powers, and its policy influence. Second was the recognition of the need for a permanent, protected, and specialized civil service. This recognition arose in some places (as in the United States) primarily from moral indignation at the corruption and excesses of political patronage, and in others primarily from the obvious necessity for adequate skills, knowledge, and experience within administration. How does one square a permanent civil service—which neither the people by their vote nor their representatives by their appointments can readily replace—with the principle of government "by the people"?

The responses to the problem took somewhat different forms and emphases in different countries, though all were essentially compatible. On the Continent, and stemming especially from Germany and Austria, the principal emphasis was upon civil law. Administration is essentially the business of carrying out the affairs of state in accordance with law and due process. The laws expressing public policies are made by the people's representatives in Parliament. In Britain, the Parliament, consisting again of elected representatives of the people, is supreme; the cabinet is a committee of Parliament, removable by the latter. The permanent British civil service consists of neutral, impartial individuals who can and will serve any cabinet with equal loyalty and devotion. In the United States, we have taken something from both camps. Our government too is conceived as one of laws rather than of men, and lawyers have long been the largest single occupational group in the top echelons of the public service. Our permanent, protected civil services, which, interestingly, do not yet include attorneys at the national level, would be impartial and neutral like their British counterpart. They would carry out policies determined elsewhere, either by the people directly (through initiative and referendum) or by their elected representatives in legislative bodies.

In short, there would be a clean division between those responsible for determining policy (the people and their elected representatives) and those responsible for carrying it out (the appointive public service).

The developments in recent decades in the "real world" of government have brought to the policy–administration dichotomy strains which have grown almost beyond the point of empirical defensibility.[2] In fact, on the theoretical plane, the finding of a viable substitute may well be the number one problem of public administration today. But this concept of dichotomy, like many others, dies hard. There are built-in obstacles of motivation in favor of perpetuating it. By and large, legislators prefer not to derogate their importance by advertising that their influence is less than it appears to be, and when they do it is often to denounce administrative (or judicial) "usurpation" of legislative power. Likewise, career administrators—especially those in specialized professions—prefer not to advertise, or even to recognize, that they are significantly influencing policy for fear of provoking such charges. And many students of government prefer to study those subjects which are amenable to scientific, objective, and quantifiable treatment, such as votes that can be counted. A declaration that these topics are somewhat less important than they seem would be self-defeating. For all three groups (elected officers, appointed administrators, and political scientists) the policy–administration dichotomy is a convenient crutch, or myth, to support and justify their current status.

Responsibility

Responsibility may well be the most important word in all the vocabulary of administration, public and private. But it

2. These developments are discussed in subsequent chapters, especially 4 and 5.

has a confusing wealth of different meanings and shades of meanings, of which I here identify two. The first, *objective responsibility*, connotes the responsibility of a person or an organization *to* someone else, outside of self, *for* some thing or some kind of performance. It is closely akin to *accountability* or *answerability*. If one fails to carry out legitimate directives, he is judged *irresponsible*, and may be subjected to penalties. In a broad sense, the dichotomy between policy and administration depends upon objective responsibility; it assumes that the administrator will carry out policy determinations decided upon elsewhere, whether or not he or she likes or approves of them. Responsibility is also essential to predictability; if a person does not behave responsibly, his or her behavior cannot be predicted.

In the classical approach to organization, objective responsibility is the first essential of hierarchy. Viewing organization from the top down, as most classicists have, we may describe the organizational process in four steps:

1. the definition and delegation of duties (i.e., responsibilities) to a subordinate;
2. the provision to said subordinate of resources (in terms of money, people, facilities, and powers) necessary to carry out such responsibilities;
3. the measurement and evaluation of accomplishments by the subordinate against assigned responsibilities;
4. the imposition of sanctions for failure to carry out responsibilities or rewards for performance beyond the "call of duty" (i.e., responsibility).

Precedent to these steps is the determination of purposes, which according to the classicists should be dictated by legislative bodies. It should be noted too that authority in this system is derivative of responsibility, not the reverse (#2). Authority should be provided from above to match responsibility—no more, no less. A great many—probably most—of the principles urged by organizational reform groups in recent decades stemmed from, or at least were consistent with, this view of responsibility in the organizational process. They include:

clear delineation of responsibilities;
responsibility to one, and only one, superior (unity of command);
delegation of authority and means for carrying out responsibilities;
reliable measurements of performance (including inspection);
rewards and sanctions appropriate to performance.

A quite different connotation attaches to the second meaning of responsibility, which is *subjective* or *psychological*. Its focus is not upon to whom and for what one *is* responsible (according to the law and the organization chart), but to whom and for what one *feels* responsible and *behaves* responsibly. This meaning is more nearly synonymous with identification, loyalty, and conscience than it is with accountability and answerability. And it hinges more heavily upon background, the processes of socialization, and current associations in and outside the organization than does objective responsibility. It introduces the possibility—indeed the inevitability—of competition and conflict among responsibilities. This was pointed out long ago by Chester Barnard, who observed that the higher an executive rose in the hierarchy, the more complex were the competing senses of responsibility to which he or she was subject.[3] Later, Arthur Maass endeavored to identify and evaluate competing objects of responsibility of administrative agencies on the basis of certain normative criteria.[4] He mentions responsibilities to:

1. the people at large (of which, as a general proposition, he disapproves),

3. In *The Functions of the Executive* (Cambridge, Harvard University Press, 1938), especially Chapter 17.
4. In Arthur Maass, "Introduction: Gauging Administrative Responsibility," *Muddy Waters: The Army Engineers and the Nation's Rivers* (Cambridge, Harvard University Press, 1951). This essay first appeared in *Public Administration Review* in 1949 under joint authorship with Lawrence J. Radway.

2. the people in pressure groups (of which, for certain limited purposes, he approves),
3. the legislature (which he feels should only be indirect through the chief executive),
4. the chief executive (which he feels should be direct),
5. a profession (for development and application of professional standards),
6. the courts (which he does not discuss).

Curiously, for a study dedicated primarily to a highly cohesive, unified body of personnel, the Corps of Engineers, Maass did not mention responsibility to the *Corps* itself, a matter which would seem of considerable importance in understanding and evaluating the behavior of its personnel.

Subjective responsibility, if one concedes its legitimacy as an element in government at all, raises immediate and obvious questions about the strength and reliability of objective responsibility. If one feels responsible in one direction (which feeling is counter to the directives received from above) and modifies his or her behavior accordingly, what reliance may be placed upon objective responsibility to the superior? A similar question may be framed to attack the underpinning of the alleged dichotomy between policy and administration. If an individual *feels* responsible in directions other than to his or her boss, or if the top boss feels responsible in directions other than carrying out legislative mandates, what assurance do we have that policy will in fact be carried out in accordance with the intention of the representatives of the people? Professional group members within agencies may embrace canons of ethics, loyalty, and responsibility to their professions which compete or conflict with expected hierarchical routines of action in specific decision situations. This special variant of the subjective–objective responsibility relationship will likely become increasingly significant as the importance of professional groups continues to grow within the public service at all levels of government. (See Chapter 5.)

Another, but closely related, version of the issue between objective and subjective responsibility was argued many years ago in an interchange of articles by Herman Finer and Carl J. Friedrich.[5] Finer placed his entire faith on objective responsibility, which he identified with democracy. "Democratic systems are chiefly embodiments of the first mentioned notion of responsibility ('objective'), and dictatorial systems chiefly of the second ('subjective')." Friedrich found this view quite unrealistic, declaring that "the responsible administrator is one who is responsive to these two dominant factors: technical knowledge and popular sentiment." He urged the necessity of professional responsibility, enforceable principally by fellow professionals and by one's own conscience. As I suggest in Chapter 5, the developments since World War II appear to give support to Friedrich's view. Our dependence upon professionals is now so great that the orientations, value systems, and ethics which they bring to their work and which they enforce on one another are a matter of prime concern to those who would strengthen the democratic system.

Representation and Representativeness

Loosely associated with the idea of subjective responsibility is that of representativeness of the people in the appointive public service. The general theme is an old one in this country. Certainly it was implicit and sometimes explicit in the Jacksonian spoils system; in the persistent opposition to a bureaucratic class; in the provision of the Pendleton Act for proportionate representation of the different states in ap-

5. Friedrich's article originally appeared in *Public Policy: A Yearbook of the Graduate School of Public Administration, 1940.* Finer's reply was published in *Public Administration Review, 1* (Summer 1941). The quotations used here are taken from longer excerpts, reprinted in Frederick C. Mosher, *Basic Literature in American Public Administration, 1787–1950* (New York, Holmes & Meier Publishers, 1981), pp. 206 and 202, respectively.

pointments in Washington; in the long-established practice of staffing most field offices with local residents. It is also reflected in the way in which administrative organizations have been structured. Most but not all interest and occupational groups have some organizational expression in the departments, agencies, bureaus, and divisions of governments, the leadership of which is expected to be responsive to the group to a greater or lesser extent. In fact, the demand of groups for representation in the structure is itself implicit acknowledgment that administration is involved in policy matters. Thus, for example, we have at the national level:

a Department of Agriculture for farmers

a Department of Labor for workers
(and a Women's Bureau for working women)

a Department of Commerce for business
(and a Small Business Administration for small businesses)

a Department of Education for educators—and students

a Veterans Administration for veterans

a National Science Foundation for scientists

a Bureau of Fish and Wildlife for sportsmen and
environmentalists and so on, almost *ad infinitum.*

In spite of these rather clear manifestations of the idea of representativeness in the public service, there has been rather little articulation of a theory of "representative bureaucracy" until quite recently. Some writers have, in the last forty years, endeavored to promote such a concept as an antidote or a supplement to legislative inadequacies and as a substitute for the shaky dichotomy of policy-politics versus administration (see Chapter 4). And it may well be that, ere long, some of the avowed political theorists will find room to discuss it in their larger discourses on political philosophy.[6]

6. In the decades of the 1960s and 1970s, there have appeared a vast array of books, monographs, and articles about or closely related to the idea of representativeness in bureaucracy. In some of these, representation and indeed participation of citizens in administrative programs affecting

But there is a confusion of at least two quite different meanings of representativeness, as there is confusion in the meanings of responsibility. First, there is an *active* (or functional) *representativeness* wherein individuals (or administrators) are expected to press for the interests and desires of those whom they are presumed to represent, whether they be the whole people or some segment of the people. Some hold that, like objective responsibility, assurance of continuing active representativeness requires some degree of answerability for decisions made and actions taken to those who are being represented. And answerability implies the possibilities of rewards for jobs well done and sanctions for failures. For the career public servant, of course, the ultimate sanction of political representatives—removal from office—is still difficult to carry out, despite recent efforts to make it more feasible. But other and more subtle rewards and sanctions are

---

them was a dominant theme, often expressed in the movement still known as "new public administration." For examples, see Frank Marini (ed.) *Toward a New Public Administration: The Minnowbrook Perspective* (Novato, Cal., Chandler, 1971); Dwight Waldo (ed.), *Public Administration in a Time of Turbulence* (Novato, Cal., Chandler, 1971); H. George Frederickson, *New Public Administration* (University, University of Alabama Press, 1980).

A second stream of literature has grown from the concern with equal opportunity, affirmative action, and discrimination against minorities, women, handicapped, and others in public employment. For examples, see the writings of Samuel Krislov, notably his *Representative Bureaucracy* (Englewood Cliffs, N.J., Prentice-Hall, 1974), and Harry Kranz, *The Participatory Bureaucracy* (Lexington, Mass., Lexington Books, 1976).

For the most part, I have refrained in this work from dealing with direct citizen participation in the conduct of government and all the myriad devices invented for that purpose—from primaries and voting to initiatives and referenda, to advisory committees, to actual delegation to citizen groups of governmental decisions. My parsimony in these areas is due to my intent to maintain a focus on the public bureaucracies themselves. Citizen participation by itself has been accorded much more extensive treatments than the one provided in this book. For a recent and excellent source, see the Advisory Commission on Intergovernmental Relations, *Citizen Participation in the American Federal System* (Washington, D.C., U.S. Government Printing Office, 1980).

possible: unfavorable publicity, reassignment, reduction of responsibilities, withholding of promotion, and others.

But there is another aspect of this subject, not necessarily related to the nature and representativeness of the career public servant. It concerns the participation of representatives of citizens in policy making and administration of programs of concern to them. Such participation and representation have become frequent, nearly standard requirements of federal programs in local areas. The potential conflicts of action and of loyalty between the local, affected representatives, and the delegated officials through established channels of local, state, and national governments are obvious.

It may be noted that active representativeness run rampant within a bureaucracy would constitute a major threat to orderly democratic government. The summing up of the multitude of special interests seeking effective representation does not constitute the general interest. The strengths of different private interest groups within administration are vastly unequal, and the establishment of anything approaching equity among them would be nearly impossible. The dangers of interest representation are reflected—perhaps excessively—in the conflict-of-interest laws. Thus there are very real problems in the development of a rounded concept of representative bureaucracy within our democratic framework.

The *passive* (or descriptive) meaning of representativeness concerns the origin of individuals and the degree to which, collectively, they mirror the whole society. It may be statistically measured in terms of locality or origin, for example, and its nature (rural, urban, suburban), previous occupation, father's occupation, education, family income, family social class, sex, race, religion. A public service, and more importantly the leadership personnel of that service, which is broadly representative of all categories of the population in these respects, may be thought of as satisfying Lincoln's prescription of government "by the people" in a limited sense. At least, such a breadth of characteristics and origins

suggests the absence of any single ruling class from which
public personnel are drawn or of any single perspective and
set of motivations. But this does not necessarily mean that a
public servant with given background and social characteristics will *ipso facto* represent the interests of others with like
backgrounds and characteristics in his behavior and decisions.
A man or woman born and bred in Ohio who takes a job in
Washington is not bound to represent the interests of
Ohioans; in fact vigorous disciplinary measures may be invoked to prevent such partiality. The same might be said of
a farmer's son or daughter or a farmer representing the interests of farmers; or of a business man, a graduate of a certain college, or a poor man or woman.

The distinction drawn here between active/functional and
passive/descriptive representativeness is by no means clear-
cut. It is rather an exaggeration of extremes. Persons drawn
from diverse groups—whether of class or income or education or race or sex or some combination of these—will bring
to bear upon decisions and activities different perspectives,
knowledge, values, and abilities. And the products of their
interaction will very likely differ from the products were they
all of a single genre. I lay stress on the distinction because it
seems to me there has been a good deal of confusion on the
matter in the recent literature about public executives. The
fact is that we know too little about the relationship between
a person's background and pre-employment socialization on
the one hand, and his orientation and behavior in office on
the other. Undoubtedly, there are a good many other intervening variables: the length of time in the organization, or
the time-distance from his or her background; the nature and
strength of the socialization process within the organization;
the nature of the position (in some, particularly among political appointees, incumbents are expected to represent
actively; in others, active representation may be expressly
forbidden and incumbents encouraged to "lean over back-

wards" to avoid the appearance of partiality); the length and content of preparatory education; the strength of associations beyond the job and beyond the agency; and others.

While passive representativeness is no guarantor of democratic decision-making, it carries some independent and symbolic values that are significant for a democratic society. A broadly representative public service, especially at the level of leadership, suggests an *open service* to which most people have access, whatever their station in life, and in which there is *equality of opportunity*. These are values which Americans have honored—in speech if not always in deed—for a century and a half. They were significant aspirations in the development of both the spoils system and the civil service system. The importance of passive representativeness sometimes resides less in the behaviors of public employees than in the fact that the incumbent employees are there at all. That is, passive representativeness has become at least symbolically crucial if not always effectively so in practice. Every federal agency and most state and local ones, for example, must now have an equal employment opportunity policy and program in place. Negatively, the significance of passive representativeness rests on the continued absence, or conspicuous underrepresentation, of certain categories of people, equal employment opportunity programs notwithstanding, suggesting barriers to their entry or advancement. Severest among the violations of passive representativeness in this country today are the shortages of women and minorities in middle and upper levels of service in most public (as well as private) agencies. (See Chapter 8.)

Mobility

A high degree of passive representativeness among the leadership personnel in government may then be construed as one index of a relatively mobile society; and if the degree of mobility in government is relatively higher than in other leadership positions in society, public employment may be considered a principal channel of, and contributor to, social mobility. There is a good deal of evidence that high mobility —accompanied as it is with concepts of equality of opportunity and an open and free society—is both widely valued in the United States and equated with democracy itself. In spite of ideologies to the contrary, Lipset and Bendix did not find social mobility, as they defined it, to be significantly higher in the United States than in many countries of western Europe, though in all it was relatively high in comparison with nonindustrial societies.[7] The studies of business and federal executives in the United States have suggested that governmental leadership reflected a somewhat higher degree of mobility than that of business, and that for both it was probably increasing.[8] All of these studies are, of course, about twenty or more years old, and there is some reason to believe that with the decline in the economic growth rate, upward social mobility has declined. Other studies have shown that upward mobility has been distinctly lower for minority races and for "outsiders"—first generation immigrants—than for others.

But there are several kinds and definitions of mobility. Sociologists, committed as many of them are to the search for vertical differentiations between classes and statuses, tend to define it in terms of shifts from one level to another. "The term 'social mobility' refers to the process by which individuals move from one position to another in society—posi-

7. Seymour Martin Lipset and Reinhard Bendix, *Social Mobility in Industrial Society* (Berkeley, University of California Press, 1959), especially Chapters II and III. I have also drawn on the work of Judah Matras, *Social Inequality, Stratification, and Mobility* (Englewood Cliffs, N.J., Prentice-Hall, 1975), which leans to a considerable extent on the Lipset-Bendix study.

8. Particularly W. Lloyd Warner, Paul P. Van Riper, Norman H. Martin, and Orvis F. Collins, *The American Federal Executive* (New Haven, Yale University Press, 1963).

tions which by general consent have been given specific hierarchical values."[9] The commonest, though admittedly an imperfect, index of rank in the social pecking order is occupation, ranging on the lower end from manual labor up through skilled labor to white collar, professional, and elite. It may be noted that a relatively high rate of upward mobility on such a scale is an inevitable accompaniment to a developing industrial society—whether it be cause or effect. As farming becomes more mechanized and more efficient, farm population declines relatively, perhaps absolutely. Mechanization and, later, automation limit the growth of manual workers in industry. Meanwhile, organizations grow, trade grows, professional services grow, management grows.

There are, however, other kinds of mobility whose importance may soon surpass upward social mobility in the economic and political world. In an increasingly specialized society—and a developing society is almost by definition an increasingly specialized one—it becomes more difficult (and more academic) to draw horizontal lines across many specialties and define vertical classes. Each specialty is likely to develop its own internal pecking order. Upward mobility within a given specialty may be both substantial and rapid if the demands for the services of that field are growing; of course, the reverse is equally true. As the educational requisites for entering a particular specialized field develop, and as career patterns within the field harden, mobility *across* specialties becomes increasingly inhibited. In other words, increasing, and increasingly specialized, education, vocationally oriented, has the double effect of facilitating upward mobility within particular fields of endeavor and discouraging interoccupational or horizontal mobility. Note that whether or not a given type of specialization has higher social standing than another may be quite irrelevant.

Another kind of mobility is that between different organi-

9. Lipset and Bendix, op. cit. pp. 1–2.

zations or different parts of the same organization: between the public and private sectors; between federal, state, city, county, and international organizations; between different agencies at the same level of government; and between bureaus, divisions, and sections of the same agency. Concern about this kind of mobility has been growing among students of public administration on two opposite grounds. First, that there is too little of it among career civil servants, the majority of whom stay in the same agencies most of their working lives and thus fail to develop the breadth and diversity of experience desirable in high-ranking executive jobs. Secondly, that there is too much of it for noncareer political appointees who stay in their government posts too short a time to learn them and to perform them well. The latter criticism applies also to members of career systems like the military and foreign services where the officers typically are assigned for relatively short tours of two to four years before being transferred elsewhere. With regard to the careerists, a wide variety of programs have been instituted to remove the obstacles and enhance the incentives for movement between private and public sectors, between different levels of government, and between and within individual agencies. Likewise, there have been efforts to encourage noncareer appointees to stay longer. But it cannot be said that either attempt has been conspicuously successful.

A related variety of mobility, sometimes a part of the same thing, is that of movement from place to place: that is, geographic mobility. In some fields of endeavor like the military and foreign services, which have already been mentioned, or like regional office managers in some federal agencies, or like city managers and public health officers among cities, there is a good deal of geographic movement. But for a large part of the public service, it is minimal. This, it is felt, contributes to a degree of parochialism of viewpoints and loyalties and behavior, and to blockages in communications and morale as among different places and between headquarters and field offices.

Finally, there is another common type of distinction in treatments of mobility: that between intergenerational mobility, measured by the difference between the vocation and status of son or daughter and parents, and intragenerational mobility, that occurring during the education and working career of a given person. The available data indicate that upward intergenerational mobility in America was relatively high, at least until quite recently, and it was somewhat higher for federal than for business executives.[10]

Employee Participation

The idea that it is desirable that members and employees of an organization take part in the reaching and carrying out of organizational decisions, which I shall call the participation hypothesis, is not a new one. Its central tenets, which go back more than two millenia, are essentially compatible in the organizational realm with democracy itself in the political realm. It has been an integral element, or at least an essential corollary, of a great many of the reform movements in the twentieth century: some versions of scientific management; industrial democracy; human relations; group dynamics; organization development; management by objectives; "new public administration." A participative system, juxtaposed against the traditional orthodoxy of authoritarian decision-making from the top down, has been advocated by a growing number of students, consultants, and practitioners in public organizations.[11] The arguments for

10. Warner et al., op. cit.
11. For a more extensive treatment of this subject as it applies to government organizations, see the cases and the analytical commentary in Frederick C. Mosher (ed.), *Governmental Reorganizations: Cases and Commentary* (New York, Bobbs-Merrill, 1967).

participative management are many and diverse, ideological and empirical:

better decisions because more knowledge and opinions would be brought to bear;

better morale and less resistance to change because employees take part in, and have a stake in, decisions;

greater degree of *self-actualization* on the part of employees, who under an authoritarian system of formal organization are treated as children and inferiors;

greater organizational *effectiveness and efficiency*;

greater degree of *commitment* to organization and larger stake in its decisions and actions on the part of employees who have actively contributed to determining its destinies;

development within organizations of the principles and ideals underlying *democracy*: respect for the dignity of the individual, egalitarianism, protection of minorities—and majorities—from arbitrary action;

employee development because of greater involvement in the work organization and setting and increased willingness to engage in job related educational programs.

The mechanics of participative democracy within an organization may include any or all of the following: collegial rather than authoritarian devices in reaching decisions; labor organization and collective bargaining; relaxing of vertical lines of authority and responsibility in formal structures; increased decentralization and delegation; permissive supervision; team building and project administration; encouragement of frank individual expression of opinions and attitudes; administration "by objective" rather than "by means" and controls; and in the extreme, actual voting on basic issues. There is neither space nor need to discuss and evaluate these types of measures here; nor need we appraise the desirability and feasibility of participative administration in organizations in general. As will be discussed later (in Chapters 5 and 6), there has already developed a great deal of collegial decision-making in many public agencies, particularly those which are largely controlled by single professional groups. But I would point out that *democracy within administration*, if carried to the full, raises a logical dilemma in its relation to *political democracy*. All public organizations are presumed to have been established and to operate for public purposes—i.e., for purposes of the people. They are authorized, legitimized, empowered, and usually supported by authorities outside of themselves for broad purposes initially determined outside of themselves. To what extent, then, should "insiders," the officers and employees, be enabled to modify their purposes, their organizational arrangements, and their means of support? It is entirely possible that internal administrative democracy might run counter to the principles and objectives of political democracy in which the organizations of government are viewed as instruments of public purpose.

The Rights and Constraints of Public Servants

The final issue concerning democracy and the public service to be mentioned here is quite different from the others. It concerns the deprivations for individual public servants of rights and privileges which other citizens enjoy, deprivations which are justified on the grounds that they are necessary to assure the continuing viability of the democratic system. The rationale for most if not all of these deprivations is commonly rooted in the concept of sovereignity, meaning essentially supremacy: The relations between the sovereign people, through the mechanism of the state, and its servants cannot be governed by the kinds of rules and practices that pervade the relations of individual citizens and their employers in the private sector of society. The sovereign will of the people must be protected, even though this may mean that the public servant must sacrifice some benefits he might otherwise enjoy. "A public job is a privilege, not a right." So runs the argument.

There are four principal kinds of programs which have operated to restrict the freedom of some, many, or all public employees:

1. the *loyalty, security, and suitability programs*, which have insisted that employees—as well as aspirants for federal jobs— be loyal to the national government and have admitted as evidences of such loyalty a variety of information as to beliefs, associations, and living habits;

2. programs to restrict *political contributions* and certain *political activities* of public employees to assure that they not utilize, nor be required to exercise, the special nature of their offices to influence partisan elections;

3. measures to ensure that public employees do not engage collectively through certain techniques, such as the *strike*, the *boycott*, and even (in some places) *collective bargaining*, in contests with their employer, the state;

4. restrictions on the private, nongovernmental interests of public employees to assure that their public powers not be utilized against the general interest, to enhance their private personal interests or other private interests which might now or later benefit them—i.e., *conflicts of interest.*

In all of the cases cited above, public employees have been specifically enjoined against practices which to most other American citizens are guaranteed by constitution or statute. There is here a curious paradox: While all of these restrictions are rationalized and defended on the grounds of democracy—government by and in the interests of the whole people—they operate to deprive a substantial proportion of all employed people of democratic rights. All of these alleged infringements have been and are under attack in various quarters. In the chapters that follow, I treat in depth only one of them—that associated with the rights to organize, bargain collectively, and employ certain weapons against the employer—i.e., the government (in Chapter 7).

2

Education and the Public Service

Some historical studies undertake broad and sweeping surveys of the evolution of total societies, focusing almost entirely upon significant events, leaders, and trends. Others are directed to the evolution of more or less specific subject areas within societies, such as education, government, or economy. This has often led to the consideration of the development of a given phase of society, with only incidental reference to the interaction of that phase with the total context in which it existed. Some recent writing about the history of education has deplored this practice in histories of education in which, it is alleged, education and particularly the formalized institutions of education have been treated as more or less separate, exogenous factors—with particular reference to American history.[1] The same difficulty has attended a good part of the writing about governmental and administrative history.

I can hardly aspire in these pages to provide any adequate treatment of the interrelationship of the history of public services with the evolution of societies. But an aspect of that interrelationship has recently come to invite inquiry by one

1. See particularly Bernard Bailyn, *Education in the Forming of American Society* (New York, Random House, 1960).

interested in the current public services: the interlocking of
the evolution of education and that of the public services,
particularly of the "elite" personnel at the higher levels. My
own inquiry was stimulated principally by three current
considerations:

1. the present-day dependence of the American public service
   upon the products, in terms both of people and of knowledge,
   of our educational institutions, particularly at the level of
   higher education; and the concurrent influence of government
   upon the educational system, its extent, and its directions;
2. the widespread differences among the higher public services
   of the United States, Great Britain, and continental Europe—
   despite the fact that all grew from origins and ideologies that
   were somewhat similar;
3. the discoveries by students of comparative administration of
   the interdependence of educational systems and their governing
   personnel, particularly in the developing countries.

It is doubtful that there is any element in an evolving culture more significant for the nature of its public service than
the educational system, both formal and informal, by which
are transmitted its ethos, frames of reference, and knowledge,
and partly through which these are changed and knowledge
is enlarged. This is not to suggest that the educational system
can be viewed as an *independent* variable operating outside
of and upon the society or its public service. It is a part of
and a respondent to its society; and, as will be shown below,
it responds to the demands of public administration while
shaping the nature of that administration. The interdependence of the educational system and the society of which it is
a part is a tautology, for the educational system is a principal
means whereby the society maintains and transforms itself.
Its influence upon government and particularly upon public
administration and the public service is immediately reflected in:

1. the degree to which public purposes are directed to the entirety
   or to special segments of the population;

2. the potential capacity for, and the limits upon, the performance of particular governmental activities;
3. the degree of democratization of the public service in the
   limited sense of providing opportunity for responsible public
   employment to a large sector of the society;
4. or, conversely, the degree to which the public service is
   stratified among particular classes of the population, themselves partly defined in terms of educational attainment;
5. the degree to which the public service can pursue technical
   and specialized programs in fields requiring particularized
   instruction and experience.

In regard to items 3 and 4, it has long been true, and it is
probably true today in virtually every country of the world,
that there exists a direct relation between the nature and the
level of educational attainment on the one hand and access to
different strata and specializations of positions in the public
service on the other. It is also true, though in widely varying
degree, that there is a relation between an individual's educational attainment and specialization and his or her economic
and social status. In other words, the educational system provides the intermediary between one's social and economic
status and one's level and influence in the society and its
government. In the long pull, change in the direction either
of democratization or of improvement of qualifications of the
public service or both cannot occur without equivalent and
usually prior changes in the educational system. This is to
say that the nature and quality of the public service depend
heavily upon the nature and quality of the system of
education.

But the proposition is equally accurate when stated in the
other direction. In modern times at least, the democratization
of education, as well as its nature (its emphasis on science,
classics, humanities, vocations, etc.), depends heavily upon
public policy and the influence of the public service. In many
societies the fundamental education is transmitted through

the family or through immediate kin. But formal and advanced education is very largely the responsibility of public agencies, whether local schools, intermediary governments (e.g., the American states and their universities), or nations. Many of the most advanced institutions of higher learning are privately endowed and governed, but even these rely on a variety of public financial aids and must acknowledge a public responsibility. Thus, while education determines, augments, and limits the potentialities of public administration, public policy to a great extent determines, augments, and limits the potentialities of education. Among modern nations, both democratic and totalitarian, there has generally been public pressure to enlarge the availability of education, to expand its reaches at higher levels, and to influence its development in specific directions of national interest. Among the developing nations, the enlargement of educational opportunities and educational specialization has increasingly been recognized as a primary requisite of modernization.

European Examples

The linking of social class with education and of education with the public service is nicely reflected in the structures of the public services as they have evolved since feudal days in western Europe. Though there are wide differences in the nature of the personnel systems of the European states, most of them were grounded in certain fundamental premises or traditions:

that the top policy-level posts, though variously defined, should be filled by politically elected or appointed and politically responsive officers;

that the remainder of the public service (except at the custodial, messengerial level) should be career personnel, selected and appointed upon completion of their education with expecta-

tion of continuing employment in their working lives in the
civil or military service and, frequently, in the agency or
ministry in which they are initially appointed;

that the career personnel should be categorized in four basic
classes, roughly matched with four levels of job responsibility
on the one hand and with classes or strata of the society,
existing now or at some time in the past, on the other;

that the basic criterion, the minimum qualification, for entry
into each class should be the level of educational attainment,
though not necessarily the field of educational specialization;

that the level of educational attainment is roughly related to the
social class in the society.

The four-class structure developed in most of the leading
nations of western Europe—Britain, France, Germany, Italy,
Austria, and Belgium—and with variations, in some of the
others. Each class had its distinctive qualification requirements, salary scale, promotion opportunities, and other familiar elements of personnel administration. Each had its
distinctive levels of duties and responsibilities to perform in
the government, though there were varying degrees of specialization within individual classes. Entry into each was
meshed in general terms with a given level of pre-entry education. To a surprising extent, the classes in these respects
were similar among the different countries, even though
there existed wide disparities in the philosophy and administration of the public service. The classes,* with their
general educational requirements and their kinds of responsibilities in government work, are listed in the accompanying table.[2]

* The titles of the classes, given here in their British names, of course differ
from country to country, though they are otherwise comparable. In France,
they are simply A, B, C, and D; in Italy, *carriere direttive, carriere di
concetto, carriere esecutive,* and *carriere del personale ausiliario;* in
Germany, *höherer Dienst, gehobener Dienst, mittlerer Dienst,* and *einfacher
Dienst.*

2. Based primarily upon Brian Chapman, *The Profession of Government*
(London, Allen & Unwin, 1959), pp. 76–77.

administrative class	university graduation	general direction, policy advice to ministers
executive class	highest level education prior to university	detailed superivision and office management
clerical class	completion of first major school examinations (age about 16)	clerical, mechanical, routine
messengerial class	primary school	messengers, porters, chauffeurs

American students may be reminded of the division of the U.S. civil service system into "services," which were abolished by the Classification Act of 1949. The old services included: (P) Professional and Scientific; (SP) Subprofessional; (CAF) Clerical, Administrative, and Fiscal; (CU) Custodial; and Clerical-Mechanical. Each had its own salary scale, though the scales were to some extent aligned with each other. But it is interesting, and probably significant of the differences between European and American views of the public services as far back as 1923 when the services were set up, that the prestigious field in this country was professional, not administrative. The respect accorded administrative work was such that it was clustered with clerical and fiscal and, in fact, listed after clerical.

The structure of the career civil services of European states mirrored the stratification of the society and, to some degree, reinforced it. Limiting the top class of career servants, who had the greatest influence on public policy and program, to graduates of universities restricted the access to influential public positions to those social and economic groups that could afford a university education. Opportunities for university education were, until quite recently, extremely restricted in Europe as they had been in the United States until the middle of the nineteenth century. The class structure of the civil services assured dominance in administration by persons from the upper class of society (which itself of course might, and indeed did, change in its constituencies). To some extent, the system provided built-in motivation for conservatism, the maintenance of the social status quo. Under the social pressure toward egalitarianism—meaning here the equalization of opportunity—and of governmental need in time of crisis, particularly war and fear of war, the stringencies of the structural barriers in the civil services were relaxed somewhat. New devices were inaugurated for the employment of specialists and professionals in fields other than the "profession of government"; opportunities for advancement from a lower to a higher civil service class were opened, though often on a temporary basis and usually with substantial restrictions.

But in the long pull the most important force toward democratizing the European public services has been, and no doubt will continue to be, the democratizing of higher education through public support of universities and fellowship programs whereby students who lack financial resources, and who come from the middle and lower social strata, may be educated. This trend toward democratization of the public service has continued in Britain, France, and some other European nations since World War II, though its manifestations and its pace have differed widely. The point is that such democratization as has occurred in the European public services has come about not primarily through modification of the structures of the public services and their entrance requirements, but mostly through modification of the educational system—its enlargement, its relaxation of social and economic requirements for admission, its financial support. Most of these changes have been state-induced and state-supported.

Yet there are very considerable differences among the public services of the European states, and these differences reflect the varying developments of their educational systems. In England, the administrative class was clearly tailored, more than a century ago, to the qualities and intellectual qualifications of the products of the two great universities, Oxford and Cambridge. The emphasis of this basic education was on the classics and the humanities, modified in recent decades by mathematics and the hard sciences. The recruiting and examining systems for the administrative class were designed to select from among the best of the products of these schools with rather little regard to the nature of their responsibilities if appointed to the public service. This was a recruitment system based upon and tailored to an elite educational system that quite deliberately accepted the content and criteria of the educational structure as qualifying for administrative appointment in the government. It had the effect, of course, of prejudicing against entry into the higher reaches of the public service those students and others experienced in the professions such as law and medicine and engineering, and students of the social sciences such as economics and government and sociology. The administrative class in Britain was predominantly a group of gentlemen, the majority of whom were products of the public schools (in the United States, private schools) and most of whom were steeped in the classical and scientific curricula of Oxford and Cambridge.[3] It represented in one sense the purest profession of governmental administrators, for it was specifically equipped for little else. On the other hand, some would doubt that it qualified as professional at all since there was little relationship between its pre-entry educational requirements and the activities it was called upon to perform. The British administrative class may perhaps best be described as a group of dedicated and highly capable "professional amateurs."

For present purposes, however, it is unnecessary to evalu-

3. For a fascinating review of the relationships between the British educational tradition and its administrative class, see Rupert Wilkinson's *Gentlemanly Power: British Leadership and the Public School Tradition* (London, Oxford University Press, 1964).

ate the British administrative class or the system whereby it was sustained. The main point is that it provided a striking illustration of the interdependence of the educational system and the nature of the public service. Revolutionary changes in education have been under way in Britain for several decades, and are contributing to basic changes in the British public service. But the interaction has gone both ways. Government, in response to social, political, and international pressures, has brought about changes in the public and private educational systems, and these changes, over a longer stretch of time, have brought about changes in the nature of the public service.

In 1968, Britain began a major and radical move away from its long-established traditions for staffing its public service. In that year, a special Committee on the Civil Service, chaired by and named for Lord Fulton, presented a report replete with recommendations, most of which were acted on.[4] In general, its thrust was away from the generalist amateurs and away from the Oxbridge monopoly. It emphasized the need for professionals and specialists, the need for trained managers, and the desirability of equitable rewards and opportunities across the board, regardless of social and educational background or field of study. Accordingly, it proposed abandonment of the traditional vertical class structure, including the administrative class, and the creation of a "classless, uniformly graded structure." It recommended a separate Civil Service Department under the Prime Minister, not the Treasury Department, and a Civil Service College. In form and in principle, most of the changes recommended by the Fulton Committee were adopted at once. The extent to which they have fundamentally modified the nature of the British civil service is still being debated. It is interesting, however, that many of the changes derived from the grow-

---

4. *The Civil Service*, Report of the Committee, 1966–68, Chairman: Lord Fulton (London: Her Majesty's Stationery Office).

ing specialisms growing out of the explosion in British higher and professional education.

On the Continent an approach developed which was more pragmatic than the British. It rested on the proposition that there are certain kinds of knowledge and subject matter which are appropriate and indeed requisite for the public official and that these may be provided by universities and other institutions of higher learning. Views as to what is the proper educational content of university programs preparatory for top positions in the public service varied in different countries and evolved over time in somewhat different ways. Most famous was the development in seventeenth- and eighteenth-century Prussia and Austria of *cameralism*, a system of higher education and merit system management designed to staff the higher civil service with men trained in what was then seen as the "stuff" of administration in a monarchical state. Chairs in cameralistics were established in a few German universities, and admissions to examination for the higher public service were for a brief period limited to graduates of programs in cameralism. The subject itself comprised those fields considered essential to the efficient management of a highly centralized, paternalistic state in an economy of mercantilism. They included predominantly what we would today refer to as public finance, including both revenue and expenditure administration, police science, and economics, with particular emphasis upon agriculture.[5] In some ways, cameralism was the principal precursor of the development of public administration in the United States in the first half of the present century, even though it had been virtually dead in Germany and Austria for nearly a century. A number of the early American apostles of public adminis-

5. According to Carl Friedrich, cameralism was also profoundly influenced by political, particularly Aristotelian, theory, the state and its bureaucracy becoming the principal agent for achieving the "common good." See his "The Continental Tradition of Training Administrators in Law and Jurisprudence," *The Journal of Modern History*, June 1939, p. 131.

tration training had studied in Germany and were influenced by the earlier German experience with cameralism, and by its subject-matter successors: political economy, administrative theory, political theory, and the beginnings of the social sciences in general.

Cameralism as a system of thought and as a method of training for public service was gradually and almost completely displaced during the latter part of the eighteenth and the first part of the nineteenth centuries by the field of law. The shift in Germany and Austria from the cameralistic to the legal approach was so profound, so extreme, and, in historic terms, so rapid as to make one wonder as to its causes. Carl Friedrich attributed it to a variety of factors: the emergence of constitutionalism and legalism to regularize the relations between states and citizens and to protect the freedom and property of the individual; the absorption of the judiciary by the monarchs; the replacement of mercantilism by the laissez-faire economics of Adam Smith and his followers; the codification of law, first in Austria, then in Germany, then under Napoleon in most of continental Europe; the conquest by the monarchs of the feudal estates; the growth of administrative, quasi-judicial tribunals; the personal predilections of individual monarchs; and others.[6]

In consequence of this shift, the content of training for the higher public service became dominantly legal, oriented not to the efficient management of the king's estate but to the proper application of law and due process. For the higher public services in Europe today, preparation remains primarily the study of law, and the great majority of administrative leaders are lawyers. However, a law program in most European universities is typically broader in scope than in England or in most law schools of the United States. It normally includes some work in what we term social science, such as economics, political science, and sociology. Legal

6. Ibid. pp. 130–47.

training for public administrators is defended not only because there is need of legal skills but also because such an education is believed to provide the habits of thought and frame of mind required by the administrative generalist. Yet, the near-monopolization of the higher civil services by legally trained officials significantly reflects a particular kind of view of the state and its role in the society as well as a particular kind of concept of the content of public administrative work. At the same time, it induces and probably perpetuates a legal method and style of decision making and of performance in public administration. The nature of this style and method is perhaps epitomized in the view, which is widely held in Germany, Italy, and some other countries, that the desirable preparation and the initial qualifications of judges and administrators are essentially comparable.[7] It is reflected in the heavy reliance, in most European ministries, upon legal codes, rules, regulations, and precedents. It is reflected in some of Max Weber's writings about legitimate bureaucracy, an idealized type which undoubtedly drew heavily upon his observations and conceptions of the German civil service.

France, with it Napoleonic rule in the early nineteenth century, its legal codification, its Conseil d'Etat, its highly centralized and rationalized administrative structure, probably had as much to do with the development of the legal tradition in the higher civil service as any other nation. Yet France never placed such exclusive reliance upon law as some other countries did, and in recent decades it has been moving farther away from it. In 1747, well before the French Revolution, the French established two of their famous technical schools, the Ecole Nationale des Ponts et Chaussées and the Ecole Nationale Supérieure des Mines, and soon after the Revolution (in 1794) they created the Ecole Polytechnique. These institutions have long been renowned for their high

---

7. See, for example, Chapman's discussion of this topic, op. cit. Chapters 2 and 3.

quality of training of engineers, scientists, and technicians, both for the military and civil services and, indeed, for private employment. All of these schools were state-owned and operated primarily to provide the state a supply of technicians who were also qualified for posts of higher management. Two years of basic scientific training in the Ecole Polytechnique was normally prerequisite for the three-year curriculum of either of the others, and these other two were the principal suppliers to the higher civil services of the engineering and technical ministries. Until the close of World War II, entry to the most responsible nontechnical posts in the French civil service—i.e., the "grands corps" (Cour des Comptes, Conseil d'Etat, and Inspection Générale des Finances) was restricted to university graduates who attained a diploma from the Ecolé Libre des Sciences Politiques, a private institution with prohibitively high fees. This effectively limited recruitment to the wealthy classes.

Comprehensive reforms, intended among other things to democratize the "grands corps" and the higher civil service generally, were instituted in 1946–47. Most celebrated among these reforms was the establishment of the Ecole Nationale d'Administration (ENA) as the sole recruiting and selecting agency for the higher civil service (other than the technicians). It was also to provide a three-year post-entry program of training and supervised experience for prospective civil servants prior to their assumption of regular government posts. Applicants for admission must have graduated from a university and most of them must have specialized in the kinds of humanistic and social subjects treated in the stiff ENA entrance examinations.[8] Training in the ENA itself is at the postgraduate level and in a fairly broad spectrum of fields considered appropriate for higher civil servants. Law, and particularly administrative law, receives less emphasis

---

8. Although some in lower divisions of the civil services are permitted to take the examination.

in the ENA examinations and in its own curricula than in some other European countries. But the legal content is there, and the legal orientation of French administration is substantial, certainly in comparison with either the British or the American governments. The most prestigious of the "grands corps" is the Conseil d'Etat; and its pièce de résistance is administrative law. The legal approach dominates others of the "grands corps" and the ministries which they administer, such as finance and even the government of the civil service itself.

Yet the ENA represents a radical departure in Europe and a significantly different approach in the relations between the educational system and the higher public service, one which has given rise to a number of somewhat different kinds of experiments in education for the higher civil services of Europe. Its effectiveness in moving toward the objective of democratizing the higher public service has, according to recent studies, been less than spectacular; progress has at best been gradual and moderate. The bulk of successful candidates still come from the upper classes, mainly in Paris, the home of the strongest university. As in all the other European countries, even including Britain, democratization of the higher public service depends basically upon extending and enlarging the opportunities for higher education. This is true in the United States as well.

The foregoing paragraphs indicate the distinguishing aspects of the higher public services in principal European countries and show, in each case, their close interconnection with the system of higher education. They fall in three main categories: the British, with their allegiance to the Oxbridge and public school tradition and their "professional-amateur" administrative class; the continental (except the French) with heavy emphasis upon law; and the French, with the long-standing institutions for post-entry instruction in technical fields, and the more recent efforts to generalize, stand-

ardize, and equalize both its selection and its training
processes for the "grands corps." All grew, in widely differing
ways, from feudal and monarchical origins. Until quite recent
times, all maintained effective dominance by the upper-
middle and upper classes of the higher public services, primarily through the intermediacy of their respective systems
of higher education. And all have, since World War II, been
the objects of reform efforts, primarily in three directions:

1. to democratize their higher civil service by opening its gates
   of entry to larger segments of the population, principally
   through democratizing higher education;
2. to strengthen their capacities to deal effectively with the social,
   economic, political, and technological problems in a period of
   accelerating change through, for example, bringing in to
   responsible positions persons educated in a variety of professional, scientific, and technical fields—in addition to law;
3. to enlarge their capabilities in the areas of administration,
   management, and broadly, politics.

The steps taken or proposed in all three of these directions in
Europe depend partly upon changes within the anatomy of
the public services themselves, but over the long pull they
depend most upon modifications of the educational systems.
It is interesting, parenthetically, that these same three subjects have been principal targets of criticism and reform
among the older *career systems* in the United States, such as
the military services and the Foreign Service. (See Chapter 6.)

The systems of higher public service described above have
of course had an influence going far beyond the shores of
Europe. They have provided the beams and girders of most
of the bureaucracies of the world—through military and
then civil occupation, through colonization, and through a
peaceful process of international osmosis consisting of technical assistance and advice, imitation, and education in one
of the institutions of a European country, whether it was
Oxford or Cambridge, the Sorbonne, Berlin, Bologna, or,
more recently, Moscow. For better or worse, the public serv-

ice systems of Europe and the educational foundations on which they are based have left an indelible impression upon most of the developing world. The military and civil services of the lesser developed nations which were once European colonies are a mixed, sometimes mixed-up, product of the imposition of the public service concepts of the imperial country upon native traditional and tribal institutions. The stamp of the British administrative-class concept continues in most of those lands which once were colored red in the atlases. And the stamp of legalism remains strong in those lands once held by continental countries. That this process did not require occupation or colonization is illustrated in the Prussian influence on the development of Japanese governmental institutions and the British and French on that of Thailand.

The American Experience

The differences between the American civil services today and their counterparts in Britain or France or Germany are, if anything, more striking than the differences among those of the three European countries which have been described above. The evolution of our interrelated systems of education and public service is particularly interesting in this regard because, through a substantial part of our history, the principal external influences upon our development were specifically England, France, and Germany in approximately that historical order. Most of the early Americans were of course themselves transplanted Englishmen who brought with them the culture, the mores, and the institutions they had grown up with. Later we were significantly influenced by and to a considerable extent dependent upon the French, particularly for engineers and technicians. Still later, our ideas about education and about public administration were heavily influenced by Germany. Yet the product, in respect both to the educational system and to the public service, is unique to America. And increasingly during the twentieth century, the flow of influence has been from America to Europe rather than Europe to America in regard to both the educational system and the public service system.

The base from which colonial America started was purely that of the mother country. After some early and largely frustrating attempts to "civilize" the natives, our forebears did not undertake to rule them, or to educate them, or to accommodate to their institutions. They pursued the simpler (and altogether disgraceful) expedient of driving them west, and in the process exterminated a great portion of them. There were of course gaping differences even among the colonists, in their cultural heritages and their attitudes—the Puritans in New England, the great planters in the South, the yeomen farmers in the mid-Atlantic states, and the gradually growing numbers of traders, merchants, and craftsmen in the seaboard cities. Yet the social system which framed the patterns of education was essentially the same as that of the mother country. The dominant element was the family, a patriarchal institution which, through kinship relationships and largely immobile geographic and vocational patterns, extended its influences to the community and its governmental institutions. Through the family were transmitted the basic values of the society: the approved patterns of behavior, the approved manners, and the approved views of the world. In addition the family, in medieval Britain and later in early America, provided the basic and sometimes the only occupational and vocational education for the young. The community in which the family resided then provided a second level of education, hardly separable, however, from the family with which it was closely related. The church provided the third major institution of education, partly through schools but also through the inculcation of moral and spiritual values and through the unifying influence of organized religion upon social integration.

An early device of more advanced vocational instruction,

developed in Great Britain and continued in America, was the apprenticeship, whereby young persons were contracted out for extended periods for training in given fields, under conditions comparable to that of the patriarchal family: the master assumed the role and the responsibilities of the father in return for training the apprentice in a given craft or trade or even profession. These institutions—the family, the community, the church, and apprenticeship—were in medieval England and in early America the primary mechanisms of education in its broadest sense—the transmission of culture and knowledge. They were augmented somewhat by formal systems of instruction in schools and universities. These institutions, however, were available only to the few. Formal education in neither the old country nor the new was a governmental enterprise, except in a spasmodic and indirect way. For the most part it was sponsored and supported by the church, by private philanthropy, and by the communities. It is interesting to note that formalized education as it developed in medieval England, and as it was brought to the American colonies, was promoted and defended because of its utilitarian services to the society of the day, not because of its broad cultural contributions. The "three Ŕ's" and elementary accounting were becoming increasingly necessary, at least among a minority of the population. Moreover, the study of the classics and Latin and Greek in the universities was essential in the training of clerics and of the increasing numbers of sons of the gentry (especially under the British primogeniture system, which caused so many second and third sons to seek public positions in the Army, Navy, and civil service). From the beginnings of the American colonies, the influential positions in our colonial public services were largely filled from upper classes who had some basis of formal education and a few of whom at least were educated at the university level in the classic subjects dominant at the English universities. This trend persisted for many generations in this country.

It is now clear that the historical bases of American education had been fundamentally modified during the colonial period to the point that, by the time of the American Revolution, we were embarked on a different path, one which would in subsequent decades sharply differentiate our public services (with a few exceptions) from those of our British forebears. Bernard Bailyn, in his perceptive interpretation of the pre-Revolutionary transformation in American education, attributes the changes to "the great axles of society— family, church, community, and the economy. . . ."[9] Basic to his thesis is the breakdown of the extended, patrilineal family, which had been brought from the "old country" and which had been predominant in basic education, not only in the teaching of the elementary subjects but more broadly in the transmission of culture from generation to generation in a stable and relatively immobile society. Under the pressure of the demands and perils of wilderness environment and a marginal economy, the family broke into relatively smaller, conjugal elements, each self-reliant and independent, few able to provide the young with the education and the security of former times. During the same period, the apprentice system, likewise inherited from England, underwent great stress and abuse and gradually disintegrated as an educational tool. Young apprentices had, in effect, been indentured out to the masters, who were obligated to take them into their families and to provide basic education as well as training in a craft. But with the scarcity of labor, apprentices were increasingly used as workmen, and the educational obligation was neglected. Early colonial laws attempted to enforce both family and master obligations for education, but without notable success.

Increasingly the colonials had to rely upon formal schooling, often conducted by the local church or its minister. But the traditional means of financing schools—principally pri-

9. Bailyn, op. cit. p. 45.

vate donations and endowments, sometimes supplemented by tuition—proved insufficient, and gradually the schools had to turn to the community for contributions and ultimately to taxation for support. By the close of the colonial period, the impetus toward a general system of free public schooling, tax-supported and locally controlled, was under way. It was a response to and a part of a broad social transformation from a tightly knit, localized society, in which various elements were mutually supportive, to one in which the individual or nuclear family had to face alone the abrasions of a harsh economy and a frontier environment, yet strove to pass along to his and her progeny such cultural and educational advantages as was possessed. Early American education was heavily religious, tied to one or another denomination, but it was also heavily utilitarian in the sense of preparing the young for vocational usefulness and advancement. The drive toward universal public education, which was one of the most prominent features of the nineteenth century and which persists, not quite fulfilled, to this day, was thus begun well before the American Revolution and was not seriously affected by that event. It made possible and probably hastened the drive toward egalitarianism, which we associate with the Jacksonians, and the accompanying doctrine that anyone (with the minimum formal education) could perform an adequate job in the civil service.

The momentum toward the egalitarian ideal contrasted sharply with the quite different character of development of higher education. For the pattern, the curricular content, and the faculties of the American colleges were singularly impervious to change until the latter half of the nineteenth century. The early American colleges—there were nine at the time of the Revolution and about twenty-five by 1800— were modeled upon their English and Scotch predecessors. Their faculties and students were male and white. Their offerings heavily emphasized theology, philosophy, the classics, and classical languages. There was some of what we would today describe as science and science investigation; but there was little vocational or professional training. Both we and the British seem to have forgotten that the medieval European universities were predominantly professional schools, directed to the "learned professions" of the ministry, law, and medicine. Most of the early American colleges were, in a sense, professional, since many of their graduates went into the ministry, and their college training had a heavy ecclesiastical flavor. Others went into other professions, but their college training was hardly directed to this end. Professional training, including legal, was largely provided by apprenticeship.

Until the second quarter of the nineteenth century, attendance was limited principally to' well-to-do children in the landed or merchant aristocracies; higher education was a monopoly of the upper class. Although some colleges aspired to attract middle- and lower-class citizens through scholarship programs, these do not appear to have been very successful; even with the scholarships, the fees were beyond the reach of the vast majority. It has been estimated that by 1800 fewer than 10,000 Americans—about two in every thousand—had been to college. By 1828, when Andrew Jackson was elected President, the number had more than doubled, but so had the population and the proportion of college graduates to population remained about the same.[10] Yet, from this tiny pool were drawn the majority of persons appointed to the top positions in the federal service, up until and including the appointments of Jackson.

During the century following the American Revolution, there was an accelerating proliferation of private colleges. Most of them were denominational, and their founding was urged by both the various churches and the states and communities of their location. They were supported also by the

10. Sidney H. Aronson, *Status and Kinship in the Higher Civil Service* (Cambridge, Harvard University Press, 1964), pp. 122–23.

drive toward egalitarian democracy, with its corollary that able young white men and, later, able women and blacks should have an opportunity for a college education. But until the Civil War there was rather little change in the concept of what the mission of the college was or, consequently, in the nature of its curriculum. There were few or no "majors," elective courses, or research, and little of what we would now call graduate work. Subject matter remained theology, philosophy, and classics with few significant invasions of the sciences. One consequence was the relative backwardness of American higher education in science for a century. A second was the separation of professional education from other higher education. The former was forced to develop through apprenticeship and later through proprietary professional schools, outside the mainstream of higher education.

The reluctance of higher education to support either science or the professions very likely contributed to the Jacksonian egalitarian philosophy of the public service. A college education was not essential to a public job, since a college education did not prepare one for any specialty. It provided culture for a gentleman, but culture was not requisite for public service. The reluctance of American colleges in the nineteenth century to prepare their students for professional and administrative work, coupled with the Jacksonian denial of careers in the public service, may well have been the death knell of any administrative class in the United States. At the same time, the conservatism of the colleges produced a vacuum which contributed to countermovements toward vocationalism during and after the Civil War.

Three major developments in the second half of the nineteenth century had fundamental influence on the subsequent development of education and the nature of the public service. One was the passage of the Morrill Act in the midst of the Civil War, which provided impetus for a host of land-grant state universities dedicated to education in "agriculture and the mechanic arts." The Morrill Act gave expression to the ethos of the nation: equality of opportunity so that most who qualified could gain higher education; faith in knowledge, rationality, and applied research to solve the problems of society; emphasis upon practicality—the study and teaching of subjects which would be helpful in carrying out occupational tasks in agriculture and industry; and a heavy orientation toward economic considerations in the subject matter of education. The Morrill Act and the federal and state actions which followed it gave emphasis to the vocational content of higher education; they thus opposed the prevailing anti-vocational tendencies. They contributed little immediately to the development of science in the universities except at a rather superficial and applied level. But over time, they provided institutional bases for scientific development and a nexus between the sciences and professional occupations. Finally, they provided the impetus and the bases whereby free, or nearly free, public higher education would later catch up with and surpass private institutions in the numbers of students.

The second major influence on higher education in the latter part of the nineteenth century stemmed from the German emphasis upon science and research and the development of the German universities as institutions for the pursuit and dissemination of knowledge, free of ideological, religious, or political bias and influence. Substantial numbers of American scholars studied in Germany during the middle and later nineteenth century, and they returned with elevated and different standards of knowledge in the various fields of learning, particularly in science. The effects included the emergence of science and research in the higher education scene; the reawakening of scholarship; and the Ph.D. degree, fiist at Yale (in 1860), then later and more importantly at Johns Hopkins (beginning in 1876), which was to become the "union card" for the profession of college-level teaching. They also included profound institutional changes: a tremendous proliferation of subject matter fields and courses; the development of the American style of "university," a mix (which is not fully digested to this day) of the older American patterns of general education of the colleges, the vocational orientation of the land-grant schools, and the emphasis from Germany upon science and research.

A third major influence on higher education was the development, in the latter part of the nineteenth century, of the public high school. Earlier the bulk of college students were in their teens, with little more than an elementary school preparation. Many of the colleges established their own academies to provide at least basic preparatory instruction for college entrance, and much of the material taught in the colleges, especially the land-grant institutions, was at a level we would today expect to be handled in the high schools. The high school curricula varied from one to four years, and most of them were considered essentially as preparatory for college; they were not conceived as terminal programs. "In 1870, for example, eight out of ten high school graduates entered college, where six of them received degrees; there were more than twice as many college graduates in the country as there were people with high school diplomas only."[11] In the years following 1880, the number of four-year high schools grew in geometric progression. By 1920, the proportion of high school graduates who went on to college fell to about 25 percent. In short, high school graduation had become terminal for the majority of students. But at the same time, the educational attainment of those who did proceed to college was greatly improved. This in turn made possible the elevation of the level of college instruction. To a very substantial degree, the rapid growth in the depth, the scope, and the numbers enrolled that has occurred in higher education since about 1880 has been made possible by the emergence of the high school.

11. Grant Venn, *Man, Education and Work: Postsecondary Vocational and Technical Education* (Washington, D.C., American Council on Education, 1964), p. 46.

With the growing support of the high schools, and under the not altogether parallel stimuli of scientism and vocationalism, American higher education burgeoned and assumed its present shape, unique in the world, during the first decades of this century. One most important dimension of this shape was the semi-independent professional school on the university campus. This development reflected—and it also conditioned—some very much larger trends in American society and culture. This was the era of progressivism in politics and of the parallel movement in the field of education also associated with the word "progressive." It witnessed the blossoming of faith in rationality, applied science, and progress. Then was the first vision of the Great Society. Scientific management grew in industry and government, as did conservation and a variety of new applied sciences in agriculture and on the countryside. A hallmark of the period, which continues to this day, was the growth of increasing specialism in the work of the nation, including that of its governments. Specialization was partly spawned and encouraged by the universities through their development of knowledge, partly forced upon them by the demands of society. But specialization on the campuses among both faculties and students became a major prop to occupational specialism on the outside, including, particularly for our purposes, specialism in the public services.

Under the onslaught of social optimism and rationality, the bastions of traditionalism—the educational institutions —had to yield some ground, though they did not do so without stubborn opposition. Vocationalism penetrated not only the universities but also the traditional liberal arts colleges and even the public schools. The Smith-Hughes Act of 1917 finally brought federal aid for vocational training below the college level, a full half-century after the Morrill Act had brought it to the universities. Professional and preprofessional educational programs began to appear in the curricula of even the most conservative four-year liberal arts colleges, a movement which has continued to this day. The general view that the educational system should aim toward the preparation of young people for their working lives as well as, or instead of, preparing them for a life of culture, took hold at all levels. The acceptance of professional training on college and university campuses was spotty, sporadic, often reluctant. But the trend was inexorable and resulted in a situation in which the bulk of higher education, undergraduate and graduate, was in fact directed to the preparation of young people for working careers. That is, it became professional.

The development of specialism and professionalism in university curricula was accompanied by a growing recognition of broadening social goals of universities in contributing to progress and in solving social problems. In the latter part of the nineteenth century, a handful of university presidents became acknowledged civic leaders and shaped some of the university programs to confront such problems—a far cry from the earlier emphasis upon the classics.[12] From its beginnings in 1876, Johns Hopkins offered studies in political economy and public administration. In 1899 the University of Chicago, then only six years old, established a college of commerce and politics to deal with, among other things, "the principal economic, social and political problems which confront the leading nations of the world."[13] In keeping with

---

12. Among those university presidents were Eliot (Harvard), Porter (Yale), Gilman (Johns Hopkins), White (Cornell), Barnard (Columbia), McCosh (Princeton), Folwell (Minnesota), and Bascome (Wisconsin). On these and related matters in these paragraphs, see Burton J. Bledstein, *The Culture of Professionalism: The Middle Class and the Development of Higher Education in America* (New York, Norton, 1976).

13. Edmund J. James, "Commercial Education" (thirteenth of the *Monographs on Education in the United States*, ed. by Nicholas Murray Butler, Louisiana Purchase Exposition Company; Albany, N.Y., J.B. Lyon Co., 1899), pp. 40–41.

this spirit, Chicago engaged Dr. Edmund J. James as Professor of Public Administration, to my knowledge the first such title in the history of the United States. During the same period, the University of Wisconsin inaugurated its program of total service to the state and society. Its president, Charles Van Hise, declared in 1905: "I shall never be content until the beneficent influence of the University reaches every family in the state. This is my ideal of a state university."[14] And Wisconsin blazed new trails in its extension program in agricultural and urban affairs, its various programs of social reform, its support of trade unionism, and its institutional economics. During the same decade, the first of this century, the most venerable institution of higher education in the country was debating a proposal for a professional school to train diplomats and civil servants. The discussions resulted, in 1908, in the Harvard School of Business, the change of focus resulting primarily because of doubts of career possibilities in the diplomatic and civil services.

The invasion of professional education on university campuses proceeded in earnest from about 1900. As late as 1895, Nicholas Murray Butler wrote that the only two professional schools of "university rank" in the United States were Harvard in law and Johns Hopkins in medicine.[15] But profound changes were taking place, changes which would revolutionize higher education in the United States:

1. the rapid development of the sciences, both social and physical, which could provide a sound basis for the development of professional training;
2. the transfer of professional education in many fields from

14. Quoted in Lawrence A. Cremin, *The Transformation of the School* (New York, Vintage Books, 1964), p. 165.
15. From his introduction to the American version of Friedrich Paulsen, *German Universities: Their Character and Historical Development* (New York, Macmillan, 1895), p. xxv.

proprietary schools and on-the-job apprenticeship to the
university campuses;

3. the birth of a number of new professions, mostly spawned on
   university campuses by providing academic substance to existing vocations. (During the first quarter of this century, systematic university training was developed, for example, in such
   fields as accounting and business education, journalism,
   nursing, optometry; further, during that period a number of
   professions developed which were more or less specifically
   directed to the public service: city planning, city management,
   diplomacy, forestry, public health, social work, teaching.);

4. the reform and upgrading of standards of professional education in the older fields—such as medicine and law—as well as
   the newer ones and the pushing of educational requirements
   up into graduate levels of instruction.

These trends, especially the first, third, and fourth, have
continued to this day. World War II and later Sputnik provided new impetus for them, especially the rapid development of the sciences. With the resulting burst of knowledge
has come the ever-growing tendency, if not the outright
necessity, to intensify specialization, to dig deeper into specialties of specialities of specialties. This has been in part a
consequence of the demands and subventions of the users of
the products of the universities: businesses and governments;
but in part it also derives from the universities themselves
and from the explosions of knowledge for which they provide
the principal fuses.

The growth of professional training on the campuses has
been the largest part of the accelerating growth in higher
education in this country. More than three fifths of all bachelor and higher degrees granted in 1977–78 were in professional fields. About one quarter were in the sciences—
physical, biological, social, and mathematical—and most of
these degree-holders no doubt proceeded to professional
careers. Only one tenth were in the humanities (arts, letters,

languages), the nineteenth-century staple of higher education, and a substantial number of these led to professional
careers, principally in teaching.[16] We have, over the course of
the last century, reversed the emphasis and the directions of
higher education: toward vocationalism and away from hu-
manism; toward specialization and away from general
culture; toward higher education as a right for those intel-
lectually capable of absorbing it rather than as a privilege for
the well-to-do; toward ascription of social status and position
on the basis of educational achievement and away from such
ascription on the basis of family background and economic
resources re-enforced and ratified by higher education.

Higher education has become the principal gateway to upward mobility in our society. As we shall see later, governmental service following such education provides a major
channel, once the gate has been passed. At the same time, the
increasing emphasis upon degrees and licenses in various
professional fields may serve to inhibit such mobility for
those still unable to attain higher education. And educational requirements in different specialized fields probably
hinder lateral movement across occupational lines. Relatively
high upward mobility provides some assurance of a representative service, in the passive sense.

The movement toward specialization and vocational preparation in higher education and, increasingly, in secondary
education has been mutually supportive of comparable
trends in government and industry. A rising proportion of
public employees are college graduates, specialized and professionally oriented, and they are providing the vast majority
of our administrative leaders below the level of political
appointments. We have no substantial "administrative class"
of cultured gentlemen as in Britain or of legally oriented

16. Source for this data is the Department of Health, Education and Welfare
National Center for Education Statistics, *Earned Degrees Conferred—
1977–1978*, (Washington, D.C., U.S. Government Printing Office, 1980),
esp. pp. 95–96, 120–24.

officials as in continental Europe. Where the problems of most European governments, and those of most of the under-developed countries as well, concern the dearth of well-qualified specialists, ours seem to be a surfeit of specialisms and professionals and a glaring need for generalists.

Finally, the growing fractionalization of specialties and the rise of organized professions have given a new cast to the older problems of policy-politics and administration, responsibility, participative democracy, and elitism. The consequences of our recent educational transformation for these issues will be considered in the chapters that follow.

3

Changing Concepts of the
Civil Service:
The First Century and a Half

The American Revolution and its concomitant successful separation of the colonies from England did not, any more than most other revolutions, eliminate traditional institutions and mores. Most of them, in the realm of government, had been brought over from the "old country" by the colonists; they survived the Revolution, and some continue to this day.[1] The ideology and practice of the early public service of the United States were clearly a heritage of our British forebears. But the Revolution occurred before the great societal and governmental upheavals in Britain and the rest of Europe, which occurred during the late eighteenth and nineteenth centuries. As has been indicated earlier, nationalist movements, the industrial revolution, and the accompanying or closely following drive toward political egalitarianism in Europe had varying, though related, effects upon the governmental systems and public services in Europeon nations. The United States, with its isolation by several thousand miles of ocean, its virtually unlimited western frontier, its vast resources inviting exploitation, and its surging population,

1. E.g., the continuing virility, in many or all states, of counties, towns, and villages, and mayors, supervisors, sheriffs, justices of the peace, coroners, and grand and petty juries.

could and did go its own way in governmental matters. One consequence was an evolution in the concept and practice of its public services entirely different from that of European countries and, as products of such evolution, a set of personnel systems, which by the mid-twentieth century were unique in the world.

For purposes of summarizing this evolution it is useful to identify certain key stages in ideology and in practice through which this country has progressed. The dates placed at the beginning and end of each stage are choices of convenience only; clearly each began before the beginning date assigned, and the influence of none of them has yet ended. Each made its special contribution to the meaning of "merit" in public employment; and each added to, and complicated, American concepts as to the proper nature and role of the public service in a democratic polity. Indeed, the principal reason for presenting them is to emphasize their continuing impact upon our values, our policies, and our practices today.

From the point of view of the public service, I divide our history into periods, listed in the accompanying table.

Period		Benchmark
1789–1829	government by gentlemen: the guardian period	inauguration of Washington
1829–1883	government by the common man: the spoils period	inauguration of Jackson
1883–1906	government by the good: the reform period	passage of Pendleton Act
1906–1937	government by the efficient: the scientific management period	founding of New York Bureau of Municipal Research
1937–	government by managers	report of Brownlow Committee

The following section explores briefly the nature and the principal lasting contributions to concept and practice of the first four of these periods. The fifth is treated in Chapter 4.

1789–1829: Government by Gentlemen

Important among the ideological bases of the American Revolution and the subsequent founding of the new government were the goals of self-government and egalitarianism among men. And important among the devices whereby equality before the government and participation in governmental decisions were to be achieved was representation of the citizenry in the policy-making offices of the government. But the Constitution provided surprisingly little guidance concerning the appointive offices of administration, other than its prescription of appointment by the President and confirmation by the Senate. George Washington, the only American president with the opportunity to build an administration "from scratch," was thus substantially free of legal prescriptions and inhibitions, as well as of the burden of past incumbencies and of organized political party pressures. He took these presidential responsibilities extremely seriously, and set the pattern of appointments to the public service which was to be followed without major change during the first four formative decades of the Republic.

In fact, Washington had rather severe limits upon his freedom, limits imposed by the nature of the society itself. The ringing words of the Declaration of Independence provided objectives and principles rather than descriptions of actuality. "All men" were far from equal in social or economic or political terms. The Congress was "representative" of much less than a majority of the adult males in the population and not of females at all. And the pool from which capable persons could be drawn to operate the administrative machinery of government was minuscule. Overall, the leadership of the administrative branch during the first quarter of our history was probably considerably less representative of the population as a whole than was the Congress.

The society of the colonies which formed the United

States was a heritage of postfeudal, preindustrial Britain. Farming was the dominant occupation, though business and trade were growing in New England and the middle Atlantic seaboard, and manufacturing, though still on a very small scale, was getting under way. Although we had forbidden the use of titles and other accoutrements of social rank, it was a highly stratified society in which wide gulfs separated the well-to-do, the middling, the poor, and the slaves. In a country in which almost nine out of every ten persons owed his livelihood to agriculture, the ownership of land was highly concentrated in a few enormous estates, except in New England.[2] The owners of the large estates and plantations, who were a minute fraction of the rural population, constituted the bulk of the de facto aristocracy in the early United States. The largest part of the rural population, however, were middle- and lower-middle-class farmers, owners of modest tracts, or tenants, but distinctly separated economically, socially, and politically from the landed gentry.

Along the seaboard, the social supremacy of the wealthy farm owners was increasingly challenged by a rising urban group of wealthy merchants and traders, although still a small minority. To these were added a small but growing number of professional men, wealthy or well-respected or both, to complete the constituency of the upper class of early America. Some of the professionals were themselves drawn from the families of the landed gentry. They included principally the clergy, lawyers, doctors, surveyors, college professors, and army officers, but in all they constituted not more than 2 percent of the employed labor force in 1800. Clearly, the pecking order of social classes in the early United States was

2. For example, it is reported that three quarters of the acreage of New York belonged to less than a dozen persons. To the south, the plantation system gradually superseded the earlier yeoman farming. I have relied heavily in this section upon Sidney H. Aronson, *Status and Kinship in the Higher Civil Service* (Cambridge, Harvard University Press, 1964). See his pages 35ff.

comparable to that in England. And, as in England, its influence penetrated virtually every aspect of American lives—
economic, political, social, educational, cultural. The "upper
crust" were, for the most part, wealthy and in positions to
influence if not dominate those in the lower classes. Despite
growing relaxation of suffrage restrictions, they pretty largely
controlled the legislative and executive positions and policies
of governments in the colonies and later in the states and the
nation.

There appears to be general agreement among historians
that George Washington and his immediate successors took
great pains to assure a high level of competence in their
appointments to the principal offices in the executive branch.
Washington himself insisted that no considerations other
than "fitness of character" should enter into his nominations
for public office, and the evidence indicates that in the main
this prescription was upheld. But the Federalist merit system
necessarily relied upon a special construction of "merit."
"Fitness of character" could best be measured by family background, educational attainment, honor and esteem, and, of
course, loyalty to the new government—all tempered by a
sagacious regard for geographic representation. After Washington came the formation of political parties, and party
identification and loyalty played an increasing role in
appointments. Yet, in spite of Jefferson's interest in broadening the democratic base of the government, the elite of the
administrative group continued to be drawn from the elite
of the society in general—from what in recent years has been
termed the "establishment." In this regard, as in so many
others, we were pursuing the habits of our English forebears.
But in sharp contrast with British practice at the time, our
early public service appears to have been remarkably free of
corruption. The business of governing was prestigious, and
it was anointed with high moral imperatives of integrity and
honor.

The early civilian public service may be considered to have

consisted of two broad categories of personnel. First were those in high-ranking offices who were in the public eye and who exercised significant influence in the making of public policy and had significant responsibility for its execution. They included the cabinet members and their ranking assistants, overseas ministers, territorial governors, bureau chiefs, chief accountants, and registers of the land offices. Appointed by the President or in a few cases by his department heads, they constituted the elite of the executive branch; they were, in today's terminology, the political executives. The second group were the workers in the offices and the field—the clerks, customs employees, surveyors, and postal emloyees. They corresponded roughly to most of those now covered in the federal civil and postal service systems. They were far greater in number of course, but much less important in shaping the directions of the new government. It should be noted that the great bulk of all employees, and particularly those in the second category, did not work in the capital but were widely scattered in the states and territories. It has been estimated that as of 1800, all but about 150 of the 3000 federal civilian employees were located in the field; that is, away from the capital.

These two categories of personnel were distinctly different, with regard not only to the content of their responsibilities but also to their social and economic origins and background, their educational attainment, and the nature of their appointments and tenure. The second category, the "workers," came very largely from the middle and upper-middle classes. Their work generally required that they have a minimum of elementary education. A few had had training or apprenticeship in a profession, such as law or medicine, and some others had specialized backgrounds in accounting or the crafts. Although the members of this group were accorded no statutory or other legal job protection, it seems to have been taken for granted from the very beginning that their tenure was for life or for the duration of their effective service. Removals in this category up to the time of Jackson were limited in number and normally justified by cause. Even under Jefferson and his successor Republican presidents, the practice of "rotation in office" did not take hold for most of the civil service. For this group, the mores and the practice of job security do not appear to have differed substantially from the legally protected security enjoyed by the present-day classified service.

The nature of the membership of the elite group in the federal service during the early period has been the object of much scholarly attention, and the evidence with regard to it is quite substantial. Perhaps the most reliable source is the statistical comparison made by Sidney H. Aronson of appointments by John Adams, Jefferson, and Jackson of persons to elite positions. Aronson's data confirm conclusively the aristocratic nature of the early federal elites. They also indicate that there was only a slight change in the direction of democratizing the higher public service by Jefferson in comparison with the Federalists and by Jackson in comparison with the Jeffersonians. Finally, they indicate that the principle and practice of tenure in office did not apply at the top level, particularly when there was a change in party control of the Presidency. Of 87 elite members appointed by Adams, 60 (more than two thirds) were original appointments—i.e., were not holdovers or reappointments from the previous administration. In the case of Jefferson, 73 of 92 elite members (nearly four fifths) were original appointments; for Jackson, 95 of 108 were original appointments—nearly nine tenths. The expectancy of job continuity of elite officeholders was, on the average, no greater then than it is for the political executives today. Obviously, there is a long precedent for the American practice of wholesale turnover of administrative leadership during political transitions.

Basing his conclusions primarily upon the occupations of fathers of elite appointees, Aronson shows that the majority of the elites of each of the three presidents came from upper-class families, but at the same time the proportions of upper-class backgrounds declined as between Adams and Jefferson and again as between Jefferson and Jackson. As might be expected from their own backgrounds and geographic residences, Adams relied more heavily upon individuals whose fathers were merchants and professionals than did Jefferson, who accorded greater priority to the sons of the landed gentry.

Table 1. Primary Occupations of Fathers of Elite Members

	Adams (N=100) %	Jefferson (N=104) %	Jackson (N=129) %
High-Ranking Occupations			
Landed Gentry	22	29	21
Merchant	22	13	17
Professional	26	19	15
Total	70	60	53
Middle-Ranking Occupations	23	25	39
Unknown	7	15	8
Grand Total	100	100	100

Note: From Aronson, 1964, p. 61. The middle-ranking category includes artisans, proprietors, farmers, teachers, sea captains, and shop or tavern keepers.

The dominance of high-ranking occupations among the elite appointees of the three presidents was even more pronounced in consideration of the primary occupations of the appointees themselves. At least 90 percent of all three groups had been engaged in the top-ranking occupations prior to their appointments, and there were no significant differences among them in this regard. The proportions of appointees in these occupations were for Adams, 92 percent; for Jefferson, 93 percent; and for Jackson, 90 percent. This suggests a substantial and rising degree of upward mobility over the course of time, or a greater disposition on the part of the later presidents to appoint "self-made" men as against those who had inherited high status, or, more likely, some of both.

1829–83: Government by the Common Man

The election of Andrew Jackson in 1828 is usually considered a turning point in the direction of American society and its government. The "reform" of the public service was only one element of a new egalitarian philosophy of society which contemplated a government "by the people" on the basis of free elections of the masses as well as the well-to-do, and administration by individuals responsive to the electorate either by frequent election or by immediate dependence upon elected officials. The tenets of the spoils system were consistent with the egalitarian ideology and may have been essential to it in the times and circumstances of mid-nineteenth-century America.

As a matter of fact, the attribution of the spoils system— together with its sorry consequences—to President Jackson is less than totally accurate. His own actions and pronouncements with regard to appointments to public office were equivocal at best.[3] In his first inaugural address, he made brief reference to the need of "reform, which will require particularly the correction of those abuses that have brought the patronage of the federal government into conflict with the freedom of elections, and the counteraction of those causes which have disturbed the rightful course of appointments and have placed or continued power in unfaithful or incompetent hands." But he followed with a promise to

---

3. The most celebrated statement—and apparently the source of the expression "spoils system"—was made by Senator William L. Marcy of New York in 1832: "They [the politicians of the United States] see nothing wrong in the rule, that to the victor belong the spoils of the enemy." (As quoted in Leonard D. White, *The Jacksonians*, New York, Macmillan, 1954, p. 320.)

"select men whose diligence and talents will insure in their respective stations able and faithful cooperation"[4] i.e., men who had a combination of merit and political loyalty. A few months later, in his first annual message to the Congress, he provided a more extended rationale for rotation in office and patronage appointments, which included virtual elimination of the merit consideration. He deplored the effects of long tenure in office, the idea of "right to official station," and the view of office as "property." But perhaps most important was the doctrine of the simplicity of public work, a doctrine which some people have not fully discarded to this day: "The duties of all public offices are, or at least admit of being made, so plain and simple that men of intelligence may readily qualify themselves for their performance; and I cannot but believe that more is lost by the long continuance of men in office than is generally to be gained by their experience."[5]

Defense of Spoils System

Yet Jackson's appointments reflected no less concern about ability and competence than did those of his predecessors. While, as noted earlier, a somewhat smaller proportion of his appointees to top-level positions were drawn from established upper-class families, he depended equally upon educated and capable men. His efforts to democratize the public service— to make it more representative of the entire population—were only moderately successful because the pool of qualified potential appointees was still limited. Actually, the percentage of office-holders whom he removed following John Quincy Adams was very nearly the same as that of Jefferson's removals following Adams' father. Clearly, Jackson did not always follow what he sometimes preached.

Jackson's view of public office as a central tenet of an egalitarian philosophy nevertheless became a symbol and guide for his colleagues and successors, not alone at the

4. James D. Richardson, (Ed.) *Messages and Papers of the Presidents,* Vol. II (Bureau of National Literature and Art, 1903), p. 438.
5. Ibid. p. 449.

national level of government but in the states and local units
as well. Among the consequences of the spoils system, run
rampant, were: the periodic chaos which attended changes in
administration during most of the nineteenth century; the
popular association of public administration with politics
and incompetence; the growing conflicts between executive
and legislature over appointments, which led in 1868 to the
impeachment trial of an American president; and the almost
unbelievable demands upon presidents—and upon executives
of state and local governments as well—by office-seekers,
particularly following elections.

The egalitarian drive which spurred and rationalized the
spoils system proved decreasingly effective as a guarantor of
popular direction and control of administration. Jackson and
his successors reduced the influence of the gentry and opened
the gates of public service to the common people. But the
new criteria for appointment produced administrations little
more representative of the whole people than before, and
now more than ever they made possible decision making
behind the scenes—"invisible government" as it was called.
Our public administration at the close of the nineteenth
century thus was little more *responsible,* in the sense of being
answerable to the whole people, than it had been at the close
of the eighteenth century. Nor was it more *responsive* to
popular needs and interests. We had effectively though not
completely transferred governmental power from one group
(the gentry) to another (the politicians); in the process, we
suffered a considerable degradation of public office and widespread corruption. We also planted the seeds for a kind of
civil service reform quite different from that instituted by
Andrew Jackson.

1883–1906: Government by the Good

Despite the sorry practices which led up to it and despite the
evangelical fervor of its advocates, the reform of the civil

service, marked by the passage of the Pendleton Act in 1883, by no means represented a complete reversal of American practice and ideology vis-à-vis public employment. It signaled a second change in direction, a change which became increasingly significant in the decades to follow; but it built upon the base which prevailed at the time, a base importantly influenced by the Jacksonian period. It did not abolish it and start anew, nor did it undertake to return to the system of the Federalists. On the contrary, civil service reform accepted the principles of egalitarianism and of equal opportunity in the public service. It sought another kind of criterion for personnel administration, which would at the same time continue to assure widespread access to public office among the citizenry. The impetus to civil service reform in this country did not derive from an effort to break a social class monopoly on the public service or to transfer civil service control from one class to another, as it had in Britain. The ideal of civil service reform in America was an open public service.

The Pendleton Act climaxed one of the most vigorous and spirited reform campaigns in American history. Protests against the spoils system had begun almost as soon as it was given a name, and efforts were made during the 1850s to require qualifying examinations for appointments, particularly to clerical positions. Taking shape in the years following the Civil War, the reform movement commanded the attention of an increasing number of public spirited civic leaders, including many in high political office.[6] Following an abortive attempt by President Grant in 1871 to set up a civil service system, civil service reform grew to become a major

---

6. The prominence of the leaders of the reform campaign, many of whom considered correction of the spoils system the principal problem of the country at the time, is suggested by the names of Carl Schurz, George William Curtis, Dorman Eaton, Richard Henry Dana, and Thomas Jenckes. Leaders during the generation following the Pendleton Act included Theodore Roosevelt and Woodrow Wilson.

political issue in the late seventies and early eighties. The enthusiasm and dedication which the movement came to command may perhaps best be explained by the fact that its essence was *moral*, at a time when American thinking was heavily moralistic. Few reform movements in American history could draw so clear a distinction between right and wrong; it was a campaign *against evils* that were clear and obnoxious.

Three interrelated consequences of the nature of the campaign that led to civil service reform may be noted. First, it associated what we now refer to as personnel administration with morality, with a connotation of intrinsic "goodness" versus "badness," quite apart from the purposes for which people were employed or the nature of the responsibilities they would carry. Second, although some protagonists mentioned efficiency as an argument for a merit system, this was at best a secondary consideration—"and not a very close second at that," to quote Paul P. Van Riper's analysis of the movement.[7] Third, it was essentially a negative movement designed to stamp out a system which was a "disgrace to republican institutions"[8]—to eradicate evil. There was not very much original thought about the best kind of substitute for spoils beyond competitive entrance examinations. Personnel administration had not yet been invented.

The Pendleton Act was inspired by the British civil service reforms which had followed the Northcote-Trevelyan report. But the products of the adaptation—the Act and its implementation—were more American than British, and they had greatly to do with the kinds of civil service systems we have today. We accepted from the British the concept of competitive examinations for entrance to public office, though the

7. In his *History of the United States Civil Service* (Evanston, Ill., Row Peterson, 1958), p. 85. See also Dwight Waldo, *The Administrative State* (New York, The Ronald Press, 1948), pp. 192ff.
8. As quoted in Waldo, op. cit. p. 192, from Dorman B. Eaton's *Civil Service Reform in Great Britain* (1879).

idea was not altogether new in our government. We also
accepted the principle of political neutrality for civil servants,
which promised a stable and continuous administrative
service free of partisan pressures and obligations. But even
these elements, adopted in principle, were modified with our
idigenous stamp. We did not divide our service into a series
of scalar classes comparable to the British four-class system
and, indeed, never seriously contemplated it. By two significant actions taken on the Senate floor during debate on the
bill, we struck down the central tenets of the closed career
system implicit in the British model. The first was the inser-
tion in the bill of a requirement that examinations be
"practical in character"—i.e., not scholarly, essay-style exer-
cises based upon academic learning but tests related immediately to the requirements of the job to be filled. An incidental
effect of this provision was to lay the basis for the
development some decades later of a detailed system of
position classification. Examinations could be made truly
"practical" only if the positions to be filled were analyzed,
described, and related to the knowledges and skills required
for them. Secondly, the Senate removed a requirement that
entrance be permitted only "at the lowest grade." It was to
be an "open" civil service with no prohibition of what we
now call lateral entry. There was provided no link between
the entrance system and the products of any particular universities, as in Britain, nor was there any link to the products
of universities in general. In fact, the bias was in quite the
opposite direction. In 1905, the Civil Service Commission in
its *Twenty-Second Report* stated that "the greatest defect in
the Federal Service today is the lack of opportunity for
ambitious, well-educated young men." It was not until the
1930s that this defect began to be remedied.

Nor did we very thoroughly emulate the British in the
matter of political neutrality. For while we did endeavor to
insulate civil servants from the hazards of patronage and
political pressures—and while we have since strengthened

the protections and inhibitions—we did not contemplate that those insulated would be in positions to direct the operations of whole agencies. We established no administrative class, no "permanent undersecretaries." Political and policy direction in the administration continued to rest in the President, his politically appointed secretaries, and the other political appointees of both, none of them protected by civil service regulations. Civil service protection pushed sporadically upward in the hierarchy, but to this day the top levels are filled by political appointees who now number two thousand or more if one liberally defines the leadership jobs.

The concept of neutrality gave the early enthusiasts for civil service reform difficulties, even as it continues to pose difficulties today. How can a public service which is neutral in political matters and which is protected be responsive to a public which expresses its wishes through the machinery of elections, political parties, and interest groups? There is no reason to doubt that the proponents of civil service reform were as vigorous in their support of popular control of government as their Jacksonian predecessors, and very likely they were just as fearful of an "entrenched bureaucracy." A possible intellectual escape[9] from this dilemma resided in the doctrine of the separation of politics and policy from administration: policy is determined by the elective representatives of the people—the legislators, the chief executive, and his politically appointed and accountable assistants; administration is the neutral execution of this policy by a competent, continuing administrative corps.

It seems significant that Woodrow Wilson, an ardent advocate of civil service reform and later a president of the National Civil Service Reform League, made the most vigorous statement on this dichotomy to that date in his remarkable essay, "The Study of Administration," in 1887, only four

---

9. I call it an "intellectual escape" because I doubt that it had much more empirical basis in the 1880s than it has today, if as much.

years after passage of the Pendleton Act.[10] Wilson saw administrative reform as the necessary sequel to civil service reform: "we must regard civil-service reform in its present stages as but a prelude to a fuller administrative reform. We are now rectifying methods of appointment; we must go on to adjust executive functions more fitly and to prescribe better methods of executive organization and action. Civil-service reform is thus but a moral preparation for what is to follow." Then he enlarged on the political neutrality theme: "Let me expand a little what I have said of the province of administration. Most important to be observed is the truth already so much and so fortunately insisted upon by our civil service reforms; namely that the administration lies outside the proper sphere of *politics.* Administrative questions are not political questions. Although politics sets the tasks for administration, it should not be suffered to manipulate its offices." This point, the apolitical nature of public adminis-tration, was the theme most stressed and probably best remembered: "The field of administration is a field of busi-ness. It is removed from the hurry and strife of politics; it at most points stands apart even from the debatable ground of constitutional study. It is a part of political life only as the methods of the countinghouse are a part of the life of society; only as machinery is part of the manufactured product."[11]

On a similar theme in 1900 Frank Goodnow wrote his famous book *Politics and Administration.*[12] The early civil service acts and the development of the civil service idea over

---

10. Woodrow Wilson, "The Study of Administration," *Political Science Quarterly*, June 1887, pp. 197–222.
11. Though, as Waldo has noted, there appears to be some inconsistency in the essay on the point. In his first paragraph, Wilson had described as the first object of administrative study to discover "what government can properly and successfully do," which sounds reasonably close to a defini-tion of policy development.
12. New York, Macmillan.

many decades depended upon and contributed to the notion that politics and policy were, or should be, separated from administration. Parenthetically, the field of public administration as a legitimate area for academic study depended heavily upon the dichotomy; most students in this field for many years hung their hats on the rack of efficiency and economy and disclaimed involvement in policy matters. A few still do.

Consistent with the ideal of political neutrality, the civil service reformers sought an organizational device which would immunize appointments and in-service activity against political influence. The civil service agency must be above and outside of the political arena—i.e., to a considerable degree independent of Congress and the Executive. To ensure its own integrity, it should be a multi-membered body representing both political parties so that no single leader or party might undermine its political neutrality. In consequence of this reasoning the civil service commission was invented. It was to become the basic model for personnel organization in the states and cities across the land, as well as a model of organization for the independent regulatory commissions which followed it. In keeping with Constitutional strictures as to the President's powers of appointment, the framers of the Pendleton Act provided that the members of the U.S. Civil Service Commission be appointed by the President with Senatorial approval, and were careful not to empower the Commission to make appointments to federal offices itself. Instead, it was to provide lists of candidates for a job "from among those graded highest" in the competitive examination, from which the appointing officer might choose. This was the basis for the "rule of three," adopted in 1888 by the Commission, given statutory legitimacy in the Veteran's Preference Act of 1944, and persisting until it was abolished by the Civil Service Reform Act of 1978.

Although the Congressional debates which preceded passage of the Pendleton Act show that some of its proponents

[margin note: Civil Service commission]

viewed the Civil Service Commission as a staff aid to the President, in practice it assumed a much more independent posture. It became an offsetting power unto itself, against political pressures from the parties, the Congress, the President, and other units in the administration. It became not alone an instrument for the orderly administration of a merit system, but a watchdog against possible transgressions against that system. In many of the states and local governments which imitated the federal civil service system, the independence and autonomy of the commissions were given an even more solid legal base. Viewed in historical perspective, the existence and the operations of the civil service commissions at all levels had two lasting effects. First, they perpetuated the association of public personnel and its administration with morality, the theme of the nineteenth-century reformers. Second, to a greater or less extent they divorced personnel administration from general management—from the executives responsible for carrying on the programs and activities of governments.

1906–37: Government by the Efficient

Civil service reform accepted without much question the Jacksonian doctrine of job simplicity. In the early years its principal targets were positions at the clerical level, and examinations were fairly elementary achievement tests. Yet, the civil service system provided a compatible base for the development during the first third of this century of technology and specialization. Its emphasis upon objectivity, upon relating qualifications with job requirements, and upon eliminating as far as possible considerations of personality and individual belief from personnel decisions was consistent with the ethos of scientific management. Further, the organizational separation and semi-independence of civil service administration provided encouragement to the development of scientific techniques in the personnel field itself.

And the doctrine of separation of policy from administration, which lent support to the ideal of a politically neutral civil service, could equally rationalize the development of a highly specialized, technically competent administration.

The development of the field (or the science, or the discipline) of public administration during this time may be regarded either as an offshoot of scientific management in the public sphere or as a similar, parallel movement. In much of their philosophy, approach, and content, the two were very nearly identical.[13] Both were grounded in a society thoroughly dedicated to growth and progress; in a philosophy of rationality; and in a faith in science and scientific method and its applicability to the practical lives of men and women, a reawakening of Auguste Comte's positivism. Both proclaimed a new gospel to the deity of efficiency. The precise meaning of the term was—and today remains—arguable, but its significance could hardly be questioned. Efficient administration was "good"; inefficient administration was "bad." It may be noted that the new "good" of efficiency did not, so far as the public service was concerned, displace the older one of a politically neutral merit system. The two deities complemented and supported each other. The public service, to be good, must be both politically neutral and efficient, and there was more than a little doubt that it could be efficient unless it was also politically neutral.

Scientific management had begun in the latter part of the nineteenth century as a bundle of techniques—loosely woven into a "philosophy"—to make industry more efficient. Later, it broadened its scope to encompass other sectors of private business and eventually parts of government. The parallel movement in public administration, starting a bit later, was seen mainly as an effort to make government more business-like; literally, more like business. The forms, structures, and

13. As Waldo has demonstrated in *The Administrative State*, Chapter 3.

procedures useful in business could be equally beneficial in government. Unlike administrative reform movements in most countries of the world, the American efficiency movement began and gained its momentum at the local rather than the national level. Its first targets were the cities, no doubt because they were the seat of most of our governmental scandals. (But there were other contributing reasons.) One was that most American government at the turn of the century was local government. In 1902, nearly three fifths of all direct public expenditures were made at the local level; and if spending related to national defense is excluded, the local portion was nearly three fourths. Another factor was that a large portion of what cities did was relatively routine, physical, and visible: maintaining and cleaning streets, supplying water, disposing of refuse, fighting fires. The principles and methods proved in business seemed readily applicable to such activities.

Public and private scientific management utilized many of the same tools and approached their problems with similar concepts. These included:

1. *rationality*: the applicability of the rule of reason, based upon research, to the organization, management, and activities of people;
2. *planning*: the forward projection of needs and objectives as a basis for work programs;
3. *specialization*: of materials, tools and machines, products, workers, and organizations;
4. *quantitative measurement*: applied as far as possible to all elements of operations, including the qualifications of individuals to do specific jobs;
5. *"one best way"*: there is one single best method of doing a job, and also one best tool, one best material, *one best type of worker*;
6. *standards and standardization*: the "one best," once discovered through systematic research, must be made the standard and thereafter rigorously followed.

All of these added up to "efficiency," meaning roughly the maximization of output for a given input, or the minimization of costs for a given output (sometimes called economy).

In its application to governmental personnel, scientific management greatly added to the substance of civil service administration. Jobs could now be studied in terms of the duties involved and the qualifications necessary to execute them; they could be systematically differentiated one from the other and standardized into classes having similar requirements. This became the basis for *position classification*. *Examinations* could be framed to measure these qualifications objectively and competitively. Merit acquired a substance beyond honesty, basic education, general intelligence, and political neutrality. Thanks in part to the aptitude testing of the U.S. Army in World War I, personnel testing by civil service organizations became perhaps the most nearly "scientific" of all activities in the personnel realm. *Training* became an approved personnel function as long as it was restricted to the provision of knowledge and skills necessary to specific classes of positions, a restriction which is still applied in many American jurisdictions. A new near-science of *efficiency ratings* was developed to provide a more objective basis for supervision and (often in conjunction with competitive examinations) as a determining force in promotions. By 1930, these activities had become the core of public personnel administration in the civil service. Among them the central hub was position classification because, according to the concepts of scientific management, the content and the requirements of the position—or class of comparable positions —controlled all the other elements in the process. Personnel administration was effectively depersonalized.

I have so far emphasized the likenesses of scientific management in the private realm and public administration in the first third of this century. But there were profound differences arising from the contexts in which the two movements grew and lived, differences of basic significance to our present understanding of democracy and the public service. Some of these arose from the nature of the auspices and leadership of the two movements. Frederick W. Taylor, the inventor of scientific management, was deeply influenced by his experience as apprentice, foreman, manager, and finally consultant for manufacturing concerns. The outlet and forum for his thoughts was initially the American Society of Mechanical Engineers. His colleagues and disciples were principally engineers and economists, both groups searching for rationality in decision making in private business. There was an underlying faith that what is good in private business (i.e., efficiency) is good for the society as a whole. But the main point here is that the stimulus and the control of management were internal; there was no suggestion in the scientific management movement that outsiders have a role in advising or directing what is "good" except through the mechanism of the market. Companies could hire good (meaning efficient) managers or they could engage private management consulting firms. But this was their option.

The development of scientific management in the governmental sphere was sparked and for several decades was powered by bureaus of municipal research, institutions unique to the public domain in this country and apparently indigenous to the United States. Beginning with the New York Bureau of Municipal Research, established in 1906, public administration assumed a quite different posture in its relation to its subject matter. The bureaus were not generated or supported *within* the public organizations they undertook to advise, nor did they sell their wisdom and services to those organizations for profit. Most of the early bureaus were privately sponsored and financed, usually by philanthropic agencies or individual philanthropists, and they derived much of their strength and influence from the very fact that they were *outside* and therefore presumably independent of government. They proceeded on the premise that the citizenry had a right, even an obligation, to know what the government was doing and how it was doing it. They could be, and often were, publicly critical of the ways in which governments conducted their business. The bureau movement from its origin invoked a sense of citizen responsibility and participation entirely foreign to the scientific management movement in private business. In the process, it attracted and recruited apostles of a quite different type. The early leaders in public administration sought efficiency, but they were also deeply committed to political democracy as they saw it. One need only read the writings of many of them —such as Allen, Bruère, Cleveland, Gulick, and Beard—to recognize the duality of their drive toward efficiency and democracy and their constant efforts to reconcile the two. Though some were trained in engineering and some in economics (and some in other fields), the underlying discipline most congenial to their views was a value-laden political science.

The disciples of the principles of scientific management in government had another difficulty to surmount: the matter of objectives. Taylor and his followers had stressed that their system would result in greater benefits and wages to the workers, greater profits to owners and investors, and, later, benefits to society in general. Its fundamental purpose from the start, however, was increased returns in relation to resources applied and this could be measured in terms of money—a criterion which was at once specific, quantifiable, and demonstrable. No such simple objective applied in most of the public sector. In the traditional lexicon of the economists, there was no market, no supply-demand relationship to determine prices, no "invisible hand" to rule out the inefficient. In the early days of the public administration movement, this problem was alleviated by the fact that most of the objectives of city governments were *givens*; products could be measured and evaluated against established purposes. Objectives were established by constitution, law, and ordinance. The job of administration was simply the carrying out, in the most efficient (or least expensive) manner, of objectives determined elsewhere. Thus was strengthened the distinction between policy and administration which had earlier supported the concept of the neutral civil service. Policy (i.e., objectives) should be determined by representatives of the people—the legislature and the chief executive; execution should be effected by efficient and neutral administrators. Perhaps the most explicit and erudite statement of this view was made by Herbert A. Simon in his first book, *Administrative Behavior*, in which he stressed the distinction of logical positivism between values (the sources of policy, which should be legislative) and facts (the basis of efficiency and the province of administration).[14] As the bureau movement grew out of its city shell and became the nucleus of a general public management movement, the handling of the objectives problem became increasingly difficult. Many of the objectives of governments other than cities were social, not readily measurable, and difficult for legislature or executive to define with any degree of exactitude.

Like other public activities during the efficiency period, the public personnel function developed and applied its own objective, scientific techniques. Also like other specialized groups, the personnelists sought separatism and autonomy in the pursuit of their discipline—protection from politicians, administrators, employees, or interest groups who might threaten professional standards. The lay civil service commission, clothed by law with power over personnel activities and endowed with a substantial degree of autonomy, provided an admirable device for insuring such protection. The commission, invented by the reformers in the nineteenth century in quite a different setting and for quite different

14. (New York, Macmillan, 1947).

reasons, provided an effective canopy for the nurture of the personnel specialisms, one which gave other professional groups in government cause for imitation.

During this period, which I call government by the efficient, civil service administration became a respected specialty, requiring focused educational background, and being divided into subspecialties. It was a near-science, an emergent profession. It treasured its techniques, its objectivity, its impersonality, its neutrality. It was not a tool of political party or pressure, of legislators or administrators. It was, or aspired to become, a triumph of technique and integrity over politics.

Recapitulation

History has obviously given the United States a mixed, cumbersome, and confusing lot of concepts about its public services. Each wave of development left lingering contributions and legacies, many of which are still operative today. Some of the more important of these are:

Government by Gentlemen: 1789–1829

the standard of "fitness of character," appraised in terms of family background, educational attainment, high ranking occupational experience

high prestige of upper-level public service

high moral standards of public office

rotation in office of public executives following party change

Government by the Common Man: 1829–1883

patronage appointments as a reward for party service

equal opportunity for public appointment, subject to party loyalty

the doctrine of simplicity of governmental work

the decline of public office and public service in popular and self-esteem

the legal profession as the source of a plurality of executive noncareer appointments

Government by the Good: 1883–1906

civil service reform as a *moral* imperative

the merit system linked primarily with competitive examinations

an "open" service, with entry possible at all levels

political neutrality of the civil service, and with it the separation of policy and politics from administration

the civil service commission to govern administration of the service—a collegial, semi-independent, nonpolitical, nontechnical body

Government by the Efficient: 1906–1937

efficiency as a second moral imperative

a science of work and management, including personnel management

position classification and the accompanying concept of rank and pay in the job rather than the incumbent

proliferation of specializations, accompanied by the development of the career idea within each.

In terms of current American concepts about the public service, the sequence of the ingredients above is as significant as the fact that they were introduced. A good many similar notions have undoubtedly influenced the development of ideology about public service in most industralized countries, but the sequence in most of them was different. Here the generally high character and caliber of the early administrations delayed the drive toward systematized merit systems. In the succeeding half century the egalitarian philosophy— centered in populism and equality of opportunity—made great strides. By the time of the Pendleton Act, a class-oriented, university-based civil service system was politically impossible. Hence ours was devised as an open system in which considerations of class or family or formal education were intentionally minimized. The corruption and scandal associated with the public service during the middle decades of the nineteenth century provided a moral groundwork for civil service reform. The reform movement implicitly relied upon a separation of politics and policy from the work of administration. The separation was urgently advocated by some, resisted by others. The scientific management movement with its emphasis on efficiency re-enforced the separation.

4

Government by Managers:
The Brownlow Report
and Its Sequels

The shift in ideological emphasis from efficiency, à la Frederick Taylor, to administrative management grew from seeds planted well before the New Deal. And management never replaced efficiency as a goal; it complemented and to some extent competed with it. Its biggest impetus was probably the Great Depression of the thirties, when it became clear that government must assume a positive role in dealing with the problems of the society and the economy. Theretofore, most of government's activities—and most thinking about its role—concerned the provision of fairly well-established services. With the New Deal, government ceased to be merely a routine servant or a passive and reactive agent. It became itself an initiator of programs and change—for a while, almost the only one. This role was strengthened during World War II when government, military and civil, dominated much of American life.

In this context, more important than efficiency in carrying out given tasks were initiative, imagination, and energy in the pursuit of public purposes. Those purposes were political, and the administrators charged with responsibility for them, as well as many of their subordinates, had to be politically sensitive and knowledgeable. Herein lay a new dimension in

83

1. efficiency is } ?
Secondary }

thinking about the public service, which neither the early reformers nor the disciples of scientific management had contemplated.

A convenient benchmark for the beginning of this period is the 1937 report by President Roosevelt's Committee on Administrative Management, better known (for its chairman) as the Brownlow Committee.[1] Perhaps the central theme of the Brownlow Committee was the concentration of authority and responsibility in the President. His _executive_ power was construed to include _administrative_ power; and administrative power, to include both the execution of established policies and initiative in developing new ones. In order to exercise these powers effectively, certain fundamental changes were necessary, and these henceforth became the orthodox commandments of public (and private) administration:

there should be clean, uninterrupted lines of direction from top to bottom, and of responsibility from bottom to top;

the President's span of control should be reduced to a manageable number by the consolidation of all administrative agencies into a limited number of departments;

independent agencies (principally the regulatory commissions) should be brought within the framework of appropriate departments for all purposes except those functions purely judicial in nature;

the President's capability with respect to his administrative responsibilities should be greatly strengthened ("the President needs help") by providing him a small White House Staff with a "passion for anonymity"; and by giving him authority over the key staff functions of fiscal management, personnel, and planning.

1. The President's Committee on Administrative Management, *Report of the Committee with Special Studies* (Washington, D.C., U.S. Government Printing Office, 1937). The members of the Committee were Louis Brownlow, Luther Gulick, and Charles E. Merriam.

At the time, there was vigorous criticism of the Brownlow report and of the bills proposed to give it effect—by legislators, the press, and by many scholars, led principally by the Brookings Institution, which denied the basic premise that the executive power encompassed the administrative power. Over the years, however, the main ideas became standard fare among most administrative reformers and students of government. A good many found their way into governmental practice. The central theses were implicit in the reports of both of the Commissions on Organization of the Executive Branch of the Government, chaired by ex-President Herbert Hoover, which reported in 1949 and 1955 respectively, in studies in the states by "little Hoover commissions," and in local-government reform movements.

Although the Brownlow Committee did not emphasize the point, the plain implication of its proposals was to lay stress upon generalist administrative qualifications for those holding intermediate and higher positions in the executive hierarchy. The Civil Service Commission had only recently opened the floodgates by providing for the recruitment and examination of college graduates on the basis of their general knowledge and intelligence for unspecified positions which were presumed to lead to administrative leadership opportunities. The National Institute of Public Affairs was recruiting interns from the colleges, and graduate training in public administration was accelerating on many campuses. There was widespread feeling against the narrowly conceived specialist and technician in administrative positions. Public administrators might or might not be trainable in administrative subject matter—the point was debated—but in any case they should be broadly educated, energetic men and women, developed through experience and protected by a merit system.

Although the management movement favored the extension of civil service coverage to the vast majority of civil positions in government, its main thrust was unfriendly to many aspects of the civil service tradition as it had developed over the years. In this respect its intent was quite opposite to that of the earlier efficiency movement. In the words of the Brownlow Committee, "Personnel administration lies at the very core of administrative management."[2] Its thrust should be positive and substantive, not negative and protective nor specialized and procedural as had been the emphasis of the predecessor civil service movements. As such its administration should be organized as a staff aid integral to the operating organization, not as a semi-independent agency. It should be headed by a single officer, appointed and removable by the executive, rather than by a collegial commission. It should operate primarily as a service to managers up and down the line, not as a watchdog and controller over management. At the top level—the level of the chief executive—it should be concerned with the development of standards and policies conducive to the effective development and execution of programs. Personnel operations, on the other hand, should be decentralized and delegated to bring them into more immediate relationship with the middle and lower managers whom they served. Personal and interpersonal considerations should be reintroduced into personal administration, even if they cost some degree of objectivity and scientific technique.

Variations on these themes found their way into many of the studies and reports during this period at all levels of government and over the years had tremendous impact upon the role of personnel administration in the total governmental process. The commission form of organization was abandoned in a great many jurisdictions in subsequent decades and ultimately in the federal government itself. During the years following the Brownlow report, changes, both in the federal and in other jurisdictions, were sporadic rather than steady, contentious rather than consensual; but

2. Ibid., p. 7.

for the most part were consistent in their direction.[3] The coverage of civil service protection was soon and vastly enlarged; position classification was extended to the field; departments and agencies were directed to set up single-headed personnel offices. Upon the recommendation of the first Hoover Commission, the chairman of the Civil Service Commission was given operational direction of the Commission's staff and became a personnel adviser to the President. And following the second Hoover Commission, attention was directed to the managerial abilities and development of the top administrative officers (see below). An early manifestation of this concern was passage of the Government Employees Training Act of 1958, which was followed in the 1960s by the establishment of several executive seminar centers and the Federal Executive Institute.

Policy and Administration Revisited

The Brownlow Committee itself seemed little troubled by the policy-politics–administration dichotomy. Within the executive branch, it sought to push the merit system upward to include "all permanent positions in the Government service except a very small number of a high executive and policy forming character. . . . The positions which are actually policy-determining, however, are relatively few in number. They consist, in the main, of the heads of executive departments, undersecretaries and assistant secretaries, the members of the regulatory commissions, the heads of a few of the large bureaus engaged in activities with important policy implications, the chief diplomatic posts. . . ."[4] A line

---

3. One should note, however, that a number of subjects which would later become major problems in public personnel administration were hardly, if at all, mentioned in the Brownlow report. These included loyalty and security, labor relations, equal employment opportunity, and conflicts of interest.

4. Ibid., pp. 7–8.

between policy-politics and administration could and should
be maintained, not as between the executive branch and the
legislature (though this position was still held at the municipal level by some city manager advocates), but as between a
handful of political appointees at the top of federal agencies
and their subordinates, almost all of whom should be in the
civil service system.

This was a convenient rationale (or rationalization), and
it was protected for the next fifteen years by the absence of a
change in party control of the Presidency. But it was less
than satisfying to the academic community, who were even
then beginning to consider policy making, if not politics, as
an integral part of administration and were working this
concept into their administration curricula. Obviously, during the New Deal period and the war which followed it, most
new policies and programs were initiated in the executive
branch, often, if not usually, well below the levels of political
appointees; obviously, too, the Congressional committees
were heavily involved in administrative detail. In the field of
government, as well as in most social sciences, academic
understanding, writing, and teaching seem to lag behind the
world of reality. Most teachers and scholars (and many others
who would become teachers and scholars) were drawn into
government service during the New Deal and the war years,
and they observed and participated in the initiating or
making of policy up and down the administrative ladders;
they also observed the interest of Congress in the details of
administration. A few might dismiss the incongruence of
what they saw with what they had taught or been taught in
the universities on the ground of emergency conditions, or
on the ground that it was "bad" government which should
be corrected as soon as possible after "that man" (Roosevelt)
in the White House was replaced. Even these must have been
disturbed later when, even after the war and after Roosevelt,
policy-politics and administration refused to sort themselves
out.

[handwritten margin note: Should be legislative]

Soon after the end of the war there began to appear a new literature which attacked the old dichotomy. Paul H. Appleby insisted that administration itself is essentially a political process—and perhaps the most important one.[5] Harold Stein directed a series of case studies whose objectives included the provision of realistic insight into the interlocking of policy and administration; the first published collection of the cases was in fact entitled *Public Administration and Policy Development*.[6] In 1954, Norton E. Long pronounced that "However attractive an administration receiving its values from political policy-makers may be, it has one fatal flaw. It does not accord with the facts of administrative life."[7]

But not all students, or public officials, or citizens, accepted the demise of the policy–administration dichotomy, nor do they today. As already noted, Herbert A. Simon gave it new life in the academic community by identifying it, more or less, with another asserted separation between values and facts; and his view has over the years influenced and motivated substantial numbers of younger social scientists to develop a "true science" of administrative decision making based upon objective facts and rational analysis, with value objectives to come from elsewhere—mainly from the people through their elected representatives. The first Hoover Commission in large part accepted and built upon the premises of the Brownlow Committee, concentrating on the orderliness and efficiency with which policies could be carried out. But the issue, which had long festered as an intellectual problem, became a thumping reality after the election of Dwight D. Eisenhower in 1952. The return of the Republicans to executive power after twenty years in the wilderness laid bare with shocking results the problems of political transition: essen-

---

5. This is his stance in virtually all of his books, including especially *Policy and Administration* (University, University of Alabama Press, 1949).

6. New York, Harcourt, Brace, 1952.

7. "Public Policy and Administration: The Goals of Rationality and Responsibility," *Public Administration Review*, 14 (1954), p. 23.

tially, how to make a public service, which was largely protected by civil service, responsive to new political leadership and different ideologies. The situation was aggravated by many factors:

over the two preceding decades, the size of the federal service had multiplied several times, and its importance in the society and its diversity and complexity had grown even more;

few Republican leaders with any federal experience were available and many of those who had worked with the Democrats were suspect in the new administration;

the great majority of federal public servants were protected under the civil service law, and a great many of them had been blanketed in, instead of entering through the approved competitive route;

the public service had itself been a target of Republican political attack during the 1952 campaign, and this attack, led by Senator McCarthy, was in fact to become more virulent during the early years of Republican leadership;

the new President, committed to a policy of retrenchment, could in only a very few cases satisfy partisan demands for jobs and power through new agencies and programs.

Among the consequences of this contretemps was a high degree of mutual suspicion between the incoming political appointees and the career officers whose activities they were intended to oversee, and, in a few agencies, an outright breakdown in communications between them. Many of the newcomers doubted that the incumbents would change their behavior in accordance with the objectives of the new administration—or could do so even if they wanted to. Some feared, and may have experienced, sabotage in the carrying out of new or changed policies. In all of this was a recognition that some protected civil servants were in positions which could influence effective public policy, even though its enunciation might come from above or from the Congress. Had the merit system been carried too far?

The new administration thought it had. Three months after his inauguration, President Eisenhower established a new category of positions unprotected by civil service (Schedule C). These would be of a "policy-determining" or "confidential" nature. In July 1953 a second Hoover Commission was established with broadened jurisdiction to consider not alone the efficiency of internal administration, like its predecessor, but also public policies. One of its principal focuses, and probably its most significant contribution, was its study of the personnel system. Its report "Personnel and Civil Service" and the accompanying task force report were the first intensive treatments of political executives, of career executives, and the relationships between the two. It was also the first major study to recommend that the number of political appointees at the top not be reduced—a reversal of a seventy-year trend. The central theme, however, did not change:

> In the 160-odd years since a two major-party system developed in the United States, the American people have sought to achieve a workable balance between two vital requirements in the management of their Federal civilian employees. One requirement, arising out of the periodic rotation of the political parties in power, is that the officials responsible for establishing and defending Government policies and programs, the noncareer executives, should be selected by the successful party. This is vital if the party is to be really accountable to the people and if it is to carry out effectively the mandates and promises upon which it is elected. The other requirement is that there must be numerous trained, skilled and nonpartisan employees in the Federal service to provide continuity in the administration of the Government's activities.[8]

8. Commission on Organization of the Executive Branch of the Government, *Personnel and Civil Service*, February 1955, p. 1.

The Commission, unlike its predecessors, undertook to spell out with precision the proper bases of distinction between executive offices which should be politically filled and those which should be filled on a career basis within the civil service system. The former should include all positions which are filled by presidential appointment; exercise statutory or delegated authority to make final decisions as to "governing policies, programs, objectives"; and require public advocacy in justifying or defending governing policies. In addition, the Commission recognized as warranting political appointments those nonexecutive positions "of a personal and confidential nature."

The Commission's task force estimated a maximum of about 800 positions which should properly qualify for political executive status. Career administrators, on the other hand, should be relieved of responsibilities for public advocacy or defense of policies and "should be kept out of direct participation in political controversies." The best of them at the top should be carefully selected and made part of a special group to be known as the Senior Civil Service, to comprise ultimately about 3000 persons.[9] These executives should be handled separately and according to quite different principles from the rest of the civil service. They should be transferable from one position to another without regard to the classification of their positions—i.e., rank was to reside in the person rather than in the job. They would have an obligation to serve "where needed most." They should be politically neutral.

This proposal of the second Hoover Commission had little immediate impact on the "real" world. Yet, its heavy emphasis upon the top groups, as distinguished from the rest of the public service, gave impetus to an unprecedented interest in

9. This was the origin of the Senior Executive Service (SES), finally legislated in 1978.

this area, which was reflected in research, writing, and action programs during the decades that followed. Its implied notion that there are identifiable, learnable principles and skills in administration as such—that an administrator can transfer from one kind of executive post to another without loss in effectiveness—capped a line of reasoning which had been developing for several decades.

Like the Brownlow Committee, the second Hoover Commission proposals drew the line not between the legislature and administration, as had the early doctrine, epitomized in the city manager plan; and not among the legislative power, executive power, and administration, as the Brookings Institution had advocated. Instead, it sought to draw the line within the executive branch itself, between those who were politically appointed and removable and those who were in the career civil service. In suggesting this division and proposing a career senior service, the Commission's report served to reignite what had become a major theme in American administrative and political theory during the period from the turn of the century up to the beginning of World War II: the proper relationship of policy and politics to administration. Indeed, scholarship on this theme during the period between the two world wars was increasing, with virtually every important scholar interested in public administration suggesting some interpretation of its scope and significance.

Prominent among the Commission's critics, predictably, were students who had already voiced their doubts that the dichotomy was or would be realistic.[10] Some feared that the senior civil service would become a built-in, protected governing elite—an administrative class (as in Great Britain) camouflaged in the garb of political innocence and policy

10. E.g., Paul H. Appleby, Stephen K. Bailey, Harlan Cleveland, Wallace S. Sayre, and Herman Somers.

neutrality. They felt that the establishment of such an elite was both contrary and threatening to the underlying principles of American democracy.

Whatever the criticism and whoever its source, however, it should be noted that the concept behind the city manager movement was, in reality, not so different from the administrative class which some so feared. That movement held that the city council would be political in the policy sense (though preferably nonpartisan), while the manager would be a trained administrator: the servant of the council to carry out its judgments, but otherwise divorced from policy. And though he or she would not be protected by civil service, each would nonetheless be appointed on the basis of his or her merit as an administrator. The city managers and their organization, the International City Management Association, have long since moved away from this extreme position with regard to the managers' proper relation to policy, but they remain almost the only generalist public administrative class in the nation.

It cannot be said that the Commission's critics came up with any very satisfactory theory to substitute for the policy-politics–administration division, but a variety of alternatives were proposed. One recognized a third category of appointive officers lying between the political appointees whose party identification is a reason and condition of appointment and the career appointees who hold permanent tenure: individuals appointed because of their competence in a given field and because they are sympathetic with the objectives of the current administration in that field. They are identified with and devoted to a particular direction in public policy. Although many are hired as career civil servants, their main careers may lie outside government. But they are not politicians either, since they are employed with little or no reference to party and they do not engage actively in politics. Some of them have been labeled "in-and-outers," available on a temporary basis as needed by an administration.

This group of policy-program, nonpolitical officers, a product of American pragmatism, gained prominence in the New Deal and has continued to be important since. Some are appointed to political office outright. Some—a much greater number—are appointed to a career service. Some are appointed in some intermediate category as consultants, or reserve officers in the military or the foreign service. Collectively, they provide a potentially significant bridge between politics and administration. But it cannot be said that they have yet been accommodated in a theory of the public service. And Heclo in his recent study of federal executives indicates that the number and influence of "in-and-outers" have been exaggerated.[11]

A second alternative to the policy–administration dichotomy was found in the *pluralism* of interests and drives among and within administrative organizations, which in turn reflected the pluralism of interests and politics in the society at large. Public administrators are heavily engaged in policy and politics a good share of their time, but much of this activity is of a different order of politics from that represented by political parties, elections, and votes in the Congress. It is controversy, competition, and negotiation among different factions within the bureaucracy itself. It consists in dealing with, responding to, or resisting clienteles and other interest groups outside the bureaucracy, and dealing with Congressional groups and other individual congressmen. From this melee, it is maintained, will emerge a degree of order and balance roughly responsive to the people expressing themselves through organized groups.

Unadulterated pluralism, however, is no guarantor of the

11. The existence and significance of this group has been recognized by a large number of students, including Paul H. Appleby, David Levitan, Herman Somers, and R.N. Spann. But Heclo's information is far more recent. See Hugh Heclo, *A Government of Strangers: Executive Politics in Washington* (Washington, D.C., The Brookings Institution, 1977) p. 102.

one-man, one-vote ideal of democracy, nor does it offer any assurance of creative development or progress. The interests of a great many people—notably minority groups and the poor—are hardly represented at all through indiscriminate pluralism. Among different agencies and programs there are vast inequalities in the outside support they can muster or the outside opposition they must resist. Furthermore, unbridled pluralism has an inescapably centrifugal effect on the structure and fabric of government. Each agency which has effective interest group support from the outside seeks autonomy to operate in its own realm; if left alone the administration responding to this drive would become a congeries of self-sufficient fiefdoms, each going its own way alone. The result would be a form of anarchy. Many administrative reformers who have recognized reality in pluralism have also recognized its limitations and dangers. The principal counteractive force against anarchy was to be the chief executive, himself elective and responsible to the whole people. They therefore strove to strengthen his position vis-à-vis the administration: through legal powers, a strong chain of command, a limited span of control, the executive budget, a vigorous body of advisers and staff units directly answerable to him.[12]

One may ask how we are to be assured that the President and his influential advisers and staff units—especially those that consist largely of career personnel—will behave responsibly for the good of the whole people. For the President, the nominating and electoral processes, the aspiration for an

---

12. The basic testament to what is now referred to as pluralism was undoubtedly the essay by James Madison published as number 10 of the *Federalist Papers* in 1787. Prominent among the current describers and advocates of pluralism is Charles E. Lindblom, who has written a number of articles and books relevant to the subject. Probably the best known of these is *The Policy-Making Process* (2nd ed., Englewood Cliffs, N.J., Prentice-Hall, 1980). A principal critic of pluralism as it has developed in this country is Theodore J. Lowi, particularly in his *The End of Liberalism: The Second Republic of the United States* (2nd ed., New York, Norton, 1979).

honorable paragraph in history, and the constraints of the next election provide some safeguards. For the political appointees, there is loyalty to the chief executive or political officers appointed by him. There is also the somewhat hopeful concept that conscientious, educated, and well-disposed public servants will behave in the general *public interest.* Though some critics have questioned the faith in, and the usefulness of, the idea of the public interest,[13] there can be no doubt that many of those who wrote about and reacted against the dangers of pluralism had faith in the public interest concept as offering a basis of viable goals. As Paul H. Appleby wrote concerning the review process of the Bureau of the Budget:

> The budget is made not merely by technical processes; it is made in a field where mighty forces contend over it. It is not made in a public arena, but the public is somehow well represented. This is one of the most mystifying of governmental phenomena.[14]

But heavy reliance upon the motivations of a relatively small group of anonymous individuals entails some confidence in their wisdom, in their humanistic upbringing and education, and in their morality. All of these became topics of great importance to those who rejected the notion that administration is or should be separate from policy, politics, and human values. Were not these high public officials a twentieth-century incarnation of Plato's philosopher-kings or of Aristotle's virtuous gentlemen?

Whether pluralism, counteracted by the chief executive and a strengthened hierarchy, sprinkled with consideration of the public interest and a touch of Platonism, constitutes an adequate theory for public administration seems a bit

---

13. See particularly Glendon R. Schubert, *The Public Interest* (Glencoe, Ill., The Free Press, 1960).

14. "The Influence of the Political Order," *American Political Science Review,* April 1948, p. 281.

doubtful. Still another ingredient—or perhaps the seed of a quite different theory—appeared during the period of government by managers: *representative bureaucracy*. The expression was used—for the first time to my knowledge—during World War II as the title of a book by J. Donald Kingsley which addressed itself to the British administrative class.[15] Among his theses were: that the British civil service reforms of the nineteenth century were intended to transfer control of the government from the aristocracy to the new business bourgeoisie; that the administrative class continued to represent the latter and to strive for the perpetuation of its values; and that this situation was the source of many of Britain's governmental deficiencies during the war years. Kingsley, in his more general analysis, declared that

> the complexity of present-day government makes it nearly impossible either for Ministers or Parliament to exercise effective control over the Service without its consent, or even without its active assistance. In England today, the bureaucracy is responsible because it is concerned with being so; and that concern is a reflection of its representative character.

And later:

> the essence of bureaucratic responsibility in the modern State is to be sought, not in the presumed and largely fictitious impartiality of the officials, but in the strength of their commitment to the purposes that the State is undertaking to serve. . . . The view of the Civil Servant as a disinterested assembler of facts simply will not stand examination.
>
> [B]ureaucracies are responsible only to the extent that they are *broadly* representative (italics mine).
>
> The influence of the bureaucracy is inescapably large in an industrial state. . . . [The British Civil Service]

15. *Representative Bureaucracy* (Yellow Springs, Ohio, The Antioch Press, 1944). Quotations from this text are from pages 274, 274–75, 279, and 281, respectively.

has been an appropriate and useful instrument of the ruling middle class and its power has been rooted in that fact—as have also its structure and ethos.

Kingsley's study, with its faintly Marxian undertones, elicited no comparable analysis in American government, perhaps because we had no such definable, homogeneous, and homogenized administrative class. He clearly merged the two meanings of representativeness that I have described in Chapter 1: representativeness of origin and background and representativeness in serving the interests of segments of the population. Here too there was probably more justification for doing so in the conservative class structure of British society than in the United States. Reinhard Bendix's study, *Higher Civil Servants in American Society*, revealed a quite remarkable degree of heterogeneity in the social backgrounds of federal executives, in striking contrast to the British and to the gentry period in our own history.[16] He concluded that "in the American setting such background factors as social origin, education, and previous career-lines fail to show a homogeneity of administrators as a group that might conceivably militate against such impartiality."[17] Bendix posed no positive theory of bureaucratic representation as an element in democracy in the modern state, emphasizing only the absence of a cohesive administrative class which might threaten democracy.

But a vaguely defined idea of bureaucratic representation crept into, or was hinted at, in a number of studies and essays during this period. Perhaps its most explicit expression was given in a series of articles between 1949 and 1954 by Norton E. Long. Long deplored the weaknesses and the irresponsible behavior of elected and partisan legislatures, and viewed the administration as an antidote: A strong bureaucracy, far from being a threat to democracy, is its greatest pillar if it is

---

16. Boulder, University of Colorado Press, 1949.
17. Ibid., p. 89.

sufficiently representative. Some of Long's points merit quotation:

> Accustomed as we are to the identification of election with both representation and democracy, it seems strange at first to consider that the nonelected civil service may be both more representative of the country and more democratic in its composition than the Congress.
>
> As it operates in the civil service, the recruitment process brings into federal employment and positions of national power, persons whose previous affiliations, training, and background cause them to conceive of themselves as representing constituencies that are relatively uninfluential in Congress. . . . the bureaucrats fill in the deficiencies of the process of representation in the legislature. . . .
>
> The democratic character of the civil service stems from its origin, income level, and association.
>
> [T]he bureaucracy now has a very real claim to be considered much more representative of the American people in its composition than the Congress.
>
> [T]he departments of administration come closer than any other organs of government to achieving responsible behavior by virtue of the breadth and depth of their consideration of the relevant facts and because of the representative character of their personnel.[18]

But Long was no mere advocate of or apologist for powerful public administrators. He described representativeness in the administration as "seriously inadequate." In another essay, he proposed that administration be deliberately structured so as to bring to bear on every policy problem proponents of differing viewpoints. He suggested building into the upper levels of the bureaucracy a "loyal opposition," com-

18. *The Polity* (Chicago, Rand McNally, 1962). The book is a collection of essays published over the previous twenty-five years. Quotations, in order of their appearance in the text, are from pages 70, 71–72, 73, 72, 92, and, in the following paragraphs, pp. 72 and 92.

parable to that found in the legislature. Recognizing and accepting the enormous power of the bureaucracy which derives from its command of facts, he proposed that it be staffed to give true expression to all major policy alternatives. This idea of building in potential opposition put him squarely at odds with the "administrative monotheism" of the first Hoover Commission—and indeed of the main thrust of the management movement as a whole.

It may be noted in passing that any theory of truly representative bureaucracy in a highly pluralistic society must also contemplate conflict within the administration as the milieu for decision making. Governmental administration would mirror all of the conflict and competition between and among the various interests and elements in the private sector. To a degree that might surprise a good many citizens, including political theorists, this has already developed in large sectors of our national administration, though not by conscious design. It is interesting that advocacy of representative bureaucracy, seen as a response to the dilemma posed by the collapse of the dichotomy of policy-politics and administration, should lead full circle to the argument that administration should be built upon internal conflict rather than upon a single, consistent, administrative hierarchy headed by the chief executive.

Finally, it may be noted that representative bureaucracy, in theory at least, introduced a quite new dimension to personnel administration, at least for some positions. If individual officers are to be chosen to represent certain interests and points of view, clearly a merit system premised on efficiency and mastery of knowledges and skills appropriate to specific jobs is not adequate. In fact, it is pretty hard to accommodate the concept of representativeness within the hard core of classification and examinations. Furthermore, can one reasonably expect an appointee, recruited early with the expectation of spending most of his working life in the public service, to continue to represent and respond to outside interests and points of view for twenty or thirty or forty years? The idea suggests a drastic modification of the career concept itself to take care of "in-and-outers" so that fresh "representatives" may be injected continuously into the flow of public administrative decision-making.

The Decade of the 1970s

Three developments of vast implications for the public services in this country occurred during the 1970s: 1. the issuance of the Model Public Personnel Administration Law in 1970; 2. Watergate; and 3. the U.S. civil service reforms, advocated by President Jimmy Carter, which became law in 1978.

The first of these, the model law, directed mainly to state and local governments, was developed, adopted, and issued by a civic organization, the National Civil Service League, and its significance requires some explanation. The National Civil Service Reform League (which several decades later dropped "reform" from its name) was established in 1881 by leaders in the civil service reform movement. The organization and those leaders were principal among the drafters of the Pendleton Act. For the following century, the League pressed for improved civil service in all jurisdictions of American government. One of its principal vehicles was publication of a model personnel law, which it revised periodically, and these models very probably had more influence on state and local personnel laws and ordinances than anything else. The first five models (the fifth was issued in 1953) continued to give considerable emphasis to the protective values of civil service against spoils and patronage and the need of collegial bodies, commissions, to prevent partisan transgressions.

In 1970, the National Civil Service League issued a new model law very different from its predecessors and quite in tune with the philosophy of the Brownlow Committee. It urged positivism rather than protectionism in civil service administration; it advocated a single personnel director, appointive and removable by the executive, with a citizen advisory board (but no civil service commission); and it encouraged a career service. It went beyond the Brownlow Committee in regard to unions and collective bargaining, relaxing restrictions on political activities, and equal employment opportunity. But its basic thrust was the same: personnel administration must be regarded as part of management, not a protector against it.

The Model Public Personnel Law of 1970 is significant for at least two conspicuous reasons. First is that it reflected the views of a great many persons—scholars, officials, civic observers—who contributed to it and approved of it. There had apparently been a sea change in the views of the cognoscenti about what the public service should be and how it should be governed. Second was that its theses were adopted by a great many state and local jurisdictions—hundreds, and perhaps by now thousands. If the Pendleton Act had been the old testament, the model personnel law became the new testament for public managers. And they were as distant from each other—and as close to each other—as the testaments in the Christian Bible. Surveys conducted by the National Civil Service League in subsequent years revealed that a very large number of state and local jurisdictions had adopted substantial portions of the proposed new model law.[19]

It seems doubtful that the Model Personnel Law had much direct influence on federal personnel practice. In the late 1950s, Senator Joseph S. Clark (D., Pa.) led a movement to

19. The text of the Model Public Personnel Administration Law together with a worthwhile critique of its tenets by Jean J. Couturier appeared in *Good Government*, Fall 1974, 91(3), p. 4ff. For a later and more complete review, see Jean J. Couturier. "The Quiet Revolution in Public Personnel Laws," *Public Personnel Management*, May–June 1976, pp. 150–67. The year of this writing (1981) is the centennial of the National Civil Service League. I must sadly report that, for want of adequate financial support, the League will probably go out of existence on this, its hundredth birthday.

establish a single personnel director under the President, but then–majority leader Senator Lyndon B. Johnson (D., Texas) never permitted it to reach the floor. The reputation of the federal service was certainly not enhanced by the Vietnam debacle, and President Nixon's proposal to establish a federal executive service in the early seventies found little favor in the Congress.

Then came the series of events which damaged the federal public service as much as anything in the previous century: Watergate. The principal targets of the Watergate investigators were the elective and appointive political officers of the executive branch (and of the Committee to Reelect the President). But however justified or unjustified they may have been, the effects of Watergate unquestionably were to tarnish the reputation of the public service in general. There were published instructions (the celebrated Malek manual) and a great many unpublished words of advice on how to circumvent civil service rules and merit principles. Very few, hardly any, career servants of the national government were directly implicated in the Watergate scandals. On the other hand, it cannot be said that many leaders or other representatives of the career services were out blowing whistles or otherwise resisting the transgressions that were being pursued. And the U.S. Civil Service Commission, which had been set up in part as a watchdog of the integrity of the civil service system, did not attack, or growl, or even bark until the affair had run most of its course.

Watergate posed in sharp relief two interrelated sets of questions about the public service. First was the relationship between the appointive political service and the career service with which and through which the former must deal. To what extent could the former rely upon the latter, especially when their perceptions of objectives differed? What should their relationships be when, as was frequently the case:

the career officers are older and more experienced than their political superiors;

the career officers have longer memories of the pasts of their
programs and greater ambitions for their futures;

the career officers have friends and associates in their professions
while their political superiors associate with politicians in
office;

the political officers seek to make their mark through quick and
dramatic changes while their career associates seek gradual
change toward long-term objectives;

loyalties differ from personal and political on one hand to
institutional and programmatic on the other hand?

But Watergate raised a larger and a harder question than
these. Oversimplified, it was whether a person, appointed by
and responsible to a leader elected by the people, should
respond to that leader or to the officials appointed by the
leader, even though these directives offended one's interests
and principles. And, in responding to such a question, should
one's answer be conditioned by whether or not he or she was
a career or a political, and therefore removable, officer?
Watergate generated doubts in the nation as a whole, not
only about the President and his immediate entourage but
about the public service as a whole, both career and noncareer. It kindled new concern about ethics in government,
about loyalty and responsibility, and about the proper roles
and relationships of political and career officials. Perhaps
most serious of all was the further loss of repute and confidence of the general public in the public services; the level
of such repute and confidence had not been very high since
the days of Andrew Jackson and in the 1970s could ill afford
further degradation.

This background may explain why Jimmy Carter as candidate for President in 1976 made reform of the federal civil
service a major plank in his campaign and why, after his
election, he appointed Alan K. Campbell, a university professor and dean of public affairs, to chair the Civil Service
Commission. The appointment was made only after both the
President and Campbell agreed and were committed to basic

changes in federal personnel management. There followed perhaps the most ambitious, far-reaching, and penetrating study of personnel practices in American history, led and conducted by experts, practitioners, and organizations both within and outside the federal establishment—more than 1500 of them. The study was accompanied by an equally ambitious program of meetings, speeches, and publicity across the land and by invitations to interest groups, scholars, business experts, and politicians for recommendations and comment. Following almost ceaseless negotiations in the executive branch, in the White House, and in the Congress, the main features of the proposed Carter personnel reforms became law in the fall of 1978.[20] They were acclaimed, perhaps prematurely, by a number of observers as the most important changes in federal personnel administration since the Pendleton Act ninety-five years earlier.

The organizational features of the reforms were: to replace the Civil Service Commission with a three-member, bipartisan Merit Systems Protection Board to handle adjudications and employee appeals, with an independent Special Counsel to investigate alleged violations of federal personnel and related laws; to establish an Office of Personnel Management (OPM) to aid and advise the President on personnel matters and to guide and coordinate the administration of the government's personnel program which would be headed by a single director and a deputy, both appointed and removable by the President; and to establish an independent and neutral Federal Labor Relations Authority to oversee, investigate, promulgate and enforce rules governing the federal labor relations program. (See Chapter 7.)

The 1978 Act added some new items to federal personnel legislation and strengthened some of the old ones. For example, the 1978 Act was the first legislation to list merit sys-

---

20. Through two separate documents: Reorganization Plan No. 2 of 1978 and the Civil Service Reform Act of 1978, P.L. 95–454, Oct. 13, 1978.

tem principles as well as prohibited personnel practices. It simplified and strengthened protections for employees against arbitrary or discriminatory actions by their superiors, including reprisals for whistle-blowing. It put new teeth into minority recruitment programs, extended the application of mobility programs with state and local governments and authorized the expenditure of funds for research and development studies and experiments in personnel administration.

But the main thrust of the Carter reforms, repeated in virtually all the speeches and arguments of their supporters, was *management*: more flexible management; better motivated management; rewards and penalties for good or bad management; development and selection of better managers; more innovative management. Here was the culminating event of "government by managers," espoused four decades earlier by the Brownlow Committee. The law and its implementing regulations are long, detailed, and enormously complex—quite beyond the space and reading time appropriate to this little book. But here is a brief outline of some of its major features:

1. A most important part of management of programs is management of the people working on those programs; authority and responsibility for people management should be vested as far as possible in those responsible for the programs, away from central personnel agencies and technicians; i.e., *decentralization*.

2. A new category of upper level administrators was created, the *Senior Executive Service* (SES), to consist of officers in the former supergrades (GS 16, 17, and 18) and in Executive Levels IV and V positions; the assignment and pay of such officials are flexible, determined by their employing agencies; exceptional performance can be recognized through salary increases and cash awards while unsatisfactory performance can be the basis of retirement or removal to a level below the SES.

3. Merit pay increases for managers and supervisors in the middle grades, GS 13–15, are likewise authorized and required.

The Reform Act of 1978 was not an omnibus bill. It left large areas of federal personnel administration untouched: recruitment and selection, classification (except for the SES, which was largely exempted), pay scales. It made some changes in veterans' preference legislation, especially with regard to veterans of the Vietnam War, but the proposed provisions to restrict veterans' benefits for older veterans were removed. Yet the Act's implementation has raised enormous difficulties as well as a good deal of resistance, especially among the SES personnel who felt cheated when Congress and the administration imposed severe cuts on their promised meritorious bonuses and pay raises. Obviously, the administration of the SES as well as the merit pay provisions for lower level administrators depend heavily upon the accuracy, reliability, and confidence attending the appraisal of employee performance. Performance evaluation has never been a strong point of federal or any other administration. The old and totally unsatisfactory system of efficiency ratings was abandoned for these employees, and each agency was instructed to develop its own system within broad guidelines issued by the OPM. The equity and employee acceptance of these many new systems remain to be seen. Further, there is doubt among some critics whether cash or salary awards (or conversely, the threat of demotion or removal) are effective motivating factors.

Finally, one must mention the effect the 1978 Act had on the roles and relationships of career and noncareer (political) officials in the SES. The Act of 1978 requires that on a government-wide basis, noncareer officers not exceed 10 percent of the SES and that 45 percent of SES positions be reserved for career personnel. But there is no further guidance as to how the two groups should relate to one another. At the time of this writing, a new administration with vastly different perceptions and ideologies has assumed power in the executive branch. It will surely present a serious challenge to the SES —its adaptability, viability, even survival.

The theme of this chapter has been *management*; it is also the central theme of the Brownlow Committee report and the central and encompassing theme of the Carter reforms of 1978. In September 1979, the Office of Personnel Management abandoned the name and content of its previous house organ, the *Civil Service Journal,* and began a new one entitled simply *Management.* In that same month, it published in another issuance an article on personnel reform which contained the key sentence: "The dominant theme in public personnel reform is to improve the responsiveness of civil service personnel to management and hence to the general public to which management is ultimately accountable."[21] This sounds very like the traditional model of what Emmette Redford has described as "overhead democracy," in which "democratic control should run through a single line from the representatives of the people . . . to their representatives in the Presidency and the Congress, and from there to the President as chief executive, then to departments, then to bureaus, then to lesser units, and so on to the fingertips of administration."[22] Redford acknowledged that the model was useful in certain ways but described it, correctly I think, as simplistic and unrealistic. Taken literally and in the light of the Watergate experience, it raises frightening questions. Does it mean that a governmental employee should take and execute instructions from above regardless of their wisdom, their legality, their morality? Should the political and the hierarchical ethic take precedence over all other norms—of conscience, or of personal or family or professional or religious allegiances? Some of these competitors for employee allegiance are discussed in succeding chapters.

21. "Common Themes in Personnel Reform," *Personnel Management Reform* (U.S. Office of Personnel Management, 1, Sept. 1979), p. 1.
22. *Democracy in the Administrative State* (New York, Oxford University Press, 1969), pp. 70–71.

5

The Professional State

There is a curious aura of unreality about much that has been said and done in the last half-century with regard to public executives and public managers. A good many otherwise enlightened citizens are not aware of their existence—other than the President, who is of course the chief executive. They know there is a chief of police and a secretary of defense and a county clerk, but these are politicians or bureaucrats, or worse, a combination of the two. They may be aware too that there is a county director of public health, a superintendent of schools, a director of the Forest Service; but these are professionals—a doctor, an educator, a forester. They are not thought of as executives or managers. And a great many of the incumbents of such positions do not think of themselves in those terms either. I have talked with a number of members of the Senior Executive Service who said that they had never thought of themselves as executives. They were engineers, biologists, lawyers, economists. They did not consider themselves managers or executives although they have made or participated in decisions affecting thousands of subordinates, millions of citizens, and sometimes billions of dollars. Some years ago, the president of one of the great universities in the world described himself in these words: "I am first of all a professor."

It may prove over the years that the greatest contributions of the Brownlow Committee on Administrative Management, the two Hoover Commissions, and Carter's personnel reform (as well as a great many other efforts) were to lend credence to the importance of what public executives were doing and therefore to the importance of selecting, preparing, and motivating them for their jobs. The faulty public image and self-image of career public servants are probably a product of developments over the last century or longer toward professionalism in American society. Although its seeds appeared earlier, the professional ethos really began to make its mark in the latter decades of the nineteenth century. It fostered, and was fostered by, a number of parallel social movements: the development of universities (or, in Clark Kerr's apt term, multiversities); increasing occupational specialism; meritocracy; careerism off the farm; the growth of an enormous, fluid, and amorphous middle class; and faith in progress.[1] In the 1960s, Daniel Bell wrote of an emerging new society in which old values and social power associated with property, wealth, production, and industry are giving way to knowledge, education, and intellect.

> To speak rashly: if the dominant figures of the past hundred years have been the entrepreneur, the businessman, and the industrial executive, the "new men" are the scientists, the mathematicians, the economists, and the engineers of the new computer technology. And the dominant institutions of the new society—in the sense that they will provide the most creative challenges and enlist the richest talents—will be the intellectual institutions. The leadership of the new society will rest, not with businessmen or corporations as we know them. . .

1. There is a growing volume of literature about the growth and effects of professionalism, mostly by sociologists. I have here relied heavily upon Burton J. Bledstein, *The Culture of Professionalism: The Middle Class and the Development of Higher Education in America* (New York, Norton, 1976).

but with the research corporation, the industrial laboratories, the experimental stations, and the universities.[2]

Viewed broadly, the professions are social mechanisms,
whereby knowledge, particularly new knowledge, is trans-
lated into action and service. They provide the means
whereby intellectual achievement becomes operational.

The extent to which the professions have become dominant in American society has been noted by a number of
commentators. Several years ago, Kenneth S. Lynn maintained that "Everywhere in American life, the professions are
triumphant."[3] And Everett C. Hughes wrote: "Professions are
more numerous than ever before. Professional people are a
larger proportion of the labor force. The professional attitude, or mood, is likewise more widespread; professional
status more sought after."[4]

In statistical terms, data of the U.S. Census and the Bureau
of Labor Statistics reflect the accelerating increase of "professional, technical, and kindred" workers, who grew from 4 to
15 percent of the American labor force between 1920 and
1978. The fastest growth has been since World War II; it
continues today and probably will do so well into the future.

The Professions and Government

The prominent role of American governments in the development and utilization of professions went largely
unnoticed for a long time. Governments are the principal
employers of professionals. According to estimates of the
Bureau of Labor Statistics, about two of every five workers

---

2. "Notes on the Post-Industrial Society," I *The Public Interest*, 6 (Winter,
   1967), p. 27.
3. Kenneth S. Lynn, "Introduction," *Daedalus*, 92 (1963), p. 649. This issue of
   Daedalus was wholly dedicated to a discussion of the development of the
   professions within America.
4. Everett C. Hughes, "Professions," *Daedalus*, 92 (1963), p. 655.

classified as "professional, technical, and kindred" (39.4%) were employed by governments in 1978, a proportion which has been stable since 1970.[5] This category does not include the multitude of engineers, scientists, and others on private rolls who are actually paid from government contracts, subsidies, and grants. Looked at another way, more than one third (36.7%) of all government employees were engaged in professional or technical pursuits, more than three times the comparable proportion in the private sector (10.9%). The governmental proportion is swollen by the education professions, especially elementary and secondary school teachers. But even if education is removed from both sides of the ledger, the percentage of professional and technical personnel in government (21.2%) is nearly double the comparable percentage in the private sector (11.6%).

Leaving aside the political appointees at or near the top of our public agencies and jurisdictions, the administrative leadership of government became increasingly professional in terms of educational and experiential backgrounds. This is not to say that public leadership as such is an administrative profession, rather that it consists of a very wide variety of professions and professionals in diverse fields, most of them related to the missions of the organizations in which they lead.

In government, the professions are the conveyor belts between knowledge and theory on the one hand, and public purpose on the other. The interdependencies of the profes-

5. Data in this paragraph are drawn from "The 1978 Class of Worker Matrix for the United States," an unpublished table furnished by the Bureau of Labor Statistics. The definition of "professional, technical, and kindred" includes occupations that some might not construe as professional, such as applied scientists, athletic coaches, embalmers, writers, artists, and entertainers. On the other hand, it excludes others that might be considered professional, including all of those who describe themselves as "managers, officials, proprietors" (of whom governments employed some 1,170,000 in 1978), military officers, and police.

sions and government are many. Governments are, or have been:

the creators of many professions;

the *de jure* legitimizers of most of those which have been legitimized;

protectors of the autonomy, integrity, monopoly, and standards of those which have such protections;

the principal supporters of their research and of that of the sciences upon which they depend;

subsidizers of much of their education;

among their principal employers and the nearly exclusive employers of some of them; which means also

among the principal utilizers of their knowledge and skills.

For their part, the professions:

contribute to government a very substantial proportion of public servants;

provide most of the leadership in a considerable number of public agencies;

through their educational programs, examinations, accreditation, and licensing, largely determine what the content of each profession is in terms of knowledge, skills, and work;

influence public policy and the definition of public purpose in those many fields within which they operate;

in varying degree and in different ways provide or control the recruitment, selection, and other personnel actions for their members;

shape the structure as well as the social organization of many public agencies.

There is nothing very new about professionalism in government. The principal spawning period for educational programs for many of the professions, as indicated in Chapter 2, was the first quarter of this century, and the U.S. Classification Act of 1923 established as the most distinguished segment a professional and scientific service. In all probability the number of professionally educated personnel in all American governments has been rising for the past century. Yet there appears to have been very little recognition of, or concern about, the significance of professionalism in the public service and its leadership until quite recently. For example, the Brownlow report and those of the two Hoover commissions, for all of their emphasis upon administrative management, paid scant attention to professionals in fields other than management as such.

The degree to which individual professional specialisms have come to dominate public agencies is suggested by the small table here. The right hand column indicates both the primary professional field in the agency and the normal professional source of its career leadership.

Federal

All military agencies	military officers
Department of State	foreign service officers
Public Health Service	public health doctors
Forest Service	foresters
Bureau of Reclamation	civil engineers
Geological Survey	geologists
Department of Justice	lawyers
Department of Education	educators
Bureau of Standards	natural scientists

State and Local

Highways and other public works agencies	civil engineers
Welfare agencies	social workers
Mental hygiene agencies	psychiatrists
Public health agencies	public health doctors
Elementary and secondary education offices and schools	educators
Higher education institutions	professors
Attorneys general, district attorneys, legal counsel	lawyers

I define the word "profession" liberally as 1. a reasonably clear-cut occupational field, 2. which ordinarily requires higher education at least through the bachelor's level, and

3. which offers a lifetime career to its members.[6] The professions in government may conveniently be divided into two classes: first, those in fields employed in the public *and* the private sectors and for whom the government must compete in both recruitment and retention. This category, which I shall call "general professions," includes most of the callings commonly understood as professions: law, medicine, engineering, architecture, and many others. I also include among them applied scientists in general and college professors. Second are those employed predominantly and sometimes exclusively by governmental agencies, which I shall call "public service professions." Most of these were generated within government in response to the needs of public programs, and although there has been a tendency in the direction of increased private employment for many of them, governments are still the predominant employers. They consist of two groups: first, those who are employed exclusively by a single agency such as military officers, Foreign Service officers, and Coast Guard officers; and, second, those employed by a number of different governmental jurisdictions, such as school teachers, educational administrators, social workers, public health officers, foresters, agricultural scientists, and librarians.

Most of those listed above in both categories may be described as "established professions" in the sense that they are widely recognized as professions, and with only a few exceptions their status has been legitimized by formal state action

6. The definition is unquestionably too loose to satisfy many students of occupations, who would like to add other requisites, such as: professional organization; or eleemosynary or service orientation; or legal establishment; or individual autonomy in performance of work; or code of ethics. In terms of governmental consequences, the liberal usage is more appropriate. For example, in terms of their group behavior in government, the officers of the U.S. Navy are at least as "professionalized" as are lawyers.

through licensing, credentialing, commissioning, recognizing educational accreditation, or a combination of these.

In addition to these professions, there are many "emergent professions" which have not been so recognized and legitimized but which are valiantly and hopefully pulling themselves up by their vocational bootstraps to full professional status. In this group are included specialists in personnel, public relations, computer technology, and purchasing. Emergent in the "public service" category are governmental subdivisions of all of these and some which are more exclusively governmental: e.g., assessors, police, penologists, employment security officers, air pollution specialists.

The professions—whether general or public service, whether established or emergent—display common characteristics which are significant for democracy and the public service. One of these is the continuing drive of each of them to elevate its stature and strengthen its public image as a profession. In a very few highly esteemed fields, such as law and medicine, the word "maintain" is perhaps more appropriate than "elevate." A prominent device for furthering this goal is the establishment of the clear and (where possible) expanding boundaries of work within which members of the profession have *exclusive* prerogatives to operate. Other means include: the assurance and protection of career opportunities for professionals; the establishment and continuous elevation of standards of education and entrance into the profession; the upgrading of rewards (pay) for professionals; and the improvement of their prestige before their associates and before the public in general.

A second common denominator of the professions is their concentration upon the *work substance* of their field, both in preparatory education and in journeyman activities, and the differentiation of that field from other kinds of work (including other professions) and from work at a lower or subprofessional level in the same field. Accompanying this emphasis upon work substance has been a growing concentration, particularly in preprofessional education, upon the sciences, which are considered foundational for the profession in question, whether they be natural or biological or social (behavioral). This emphasis is an inevitable consequence of the explosive developments of science in the last several decades, and unquestionably it has contributed to the betterment of professional performance in the technical sense.

Partially in consequence of the concentration upon science and work substance there has been a much less than parallel treatment of the *ecology* of the profession in the total social milieu: of the consequences and purposes of the profession and of the constraints within which it operates. There are signs in a good many fields today that attention to these topics is increasing, particularly in the public service professions. Yet much of professional education and practice is still so focused on substance and science as to obscure the larger meaning of the profession in the society. Except for those few professionals who grow beyond their field, the real world is seen as by a submariner through a periscope whose direction and focus are fixed.

One of the most obscure sectors of the real world in professional education and much of its practice is the realm of government and politics. There is a built-in animosity between the professions and politics. Its origin is historical: Most of the professions, and particularly those in the public service category, won their professional spurs over many arduous years of contending against the infiltration, the domination, and the influence of politicians (who to many professionals are amateurs at best and criminals at worst). Compare, for example, the evolution of such fields as the military, diplomacy, social welfare, and city management. The aversion to politics also has contemporary support. Professionalism rests upon specialized knowledge, science, and rationality. There are *correct* ways of solving problems and doing things. Politics is seen as being engaged in the fuzzy areas of negotiation, elections, votes, compromises—all carried on by subject-matter amateurs. Politics is to the professions as ambiguity to truth, expediency to rightness, heresy to true belief.

Government as a whole comes off not much better than politics in the eyes of most professions, particularly the "general" ones. By definition, it carries the political taint. It also violates or threatens some of the treasured attributes and myths of true professionalism: individual and professional autonomy, and freedom from "bureaucratic" control; service to, and fees from, individual clients; vocational self-government. Among those general professions with large numbers of members employed privately, preservice education usually treats government as an outside agency with or against which one must deal. This seems to be true of most education in law, engineering, accounting, and other business fields, upon which government is heavily dependent. It is also true of medicine and most of its subspecialties. Even in many public service professions—public school education provides an excellent example—there is a considerable aversion to government *in general* and to politics, which may be another word for the same thing. Government is all right in those particular areas in which the specified profession has dominant control; but beyond those perimeters, it is equated with "politics" and "bureaucracy" in their more invidious senses.

I doubt that it is appropriate to speak of "strategies" of the professions in government, because some of their consequences seem to have "just growed" rather than to have been consciously planned. Yet those consequences are fairly consistent, particularly among the established professions, whether of the public service or the general category. And the emergent professions are varying distances down the road. The pattern has these features:

1. the given profession has staked its territory within the appropriate governmental agency or agencies, usually with

boundaries approximately coterminous with those of the organization itself;
2. within its organization, it has formed an elite corps with substantial control over the operations of the agency, significant influence on agency policies, and high prestige within and outside the agency;
3. to the extent possible, it has assumed control over employment policies and individual personnel actions for its own members in the agency and also over the employment of persons not in the elite profession;
4. it has provided its members the opportunities, assurances, and protections of a career system of employment.

The following two sections will deal with items 2 and 3 above. Item 4, career systems, is treated in Chapter 6.

Professional Elites

Our study and hence our understanding of public administrative organizations have for some time been conditioned by two primary considerations. One is simply the past, when most organizations were not professionalized and when it seemed logical to build on the premise that organization consisted of two essential elements: management and workers. The focus was upon the problems, the skills, the content of management viewed as a single, common task, regardless of the differing activities and objectives of the organizations.[7] The second source of our lore about public organizations derives principally from studies of organizations in the realm of private business, but augmented by cases and analyses about some public or semi-public organizations usually at a fairly subordinate level of operations: military units, hospitals, mental institutions, prisons, schools, and scientific laboratories. The more recent of the organizational literature

7. For examples see the works of Frederick Taylor, Henri Fayol, or Chester Barnard. Their main tenets were reinforced by the writings of Max Weber.

has recognized and even dwelt upon a third element of organization: the professionals, usually viewed as *staff*. They are organizationally below management but are often considered to be superior in educational and social terms.

So we begin our organizational analysis from a *trichotomy* which consists of management, workers, and professionals or staff. The professionals are categorized according to whether they are dedicated to their organizations (the "locals") or to their professions (the "cosmopolitans"). There are presumed conflicts of prospects and goals between management and workers, between professionals and workers, and between management and professionals.

One hesitates to generalize as to the validity or usefulness of either the dichotomous or the trichotomous premises in nonpublic organization today. Undoubtedly they are still applicable in many industrial and commercial organizations. They seem quite inapplicable, however, in most of the professionalized agencies of government, and these include the most important ones. In these agencies:

the managers are professionals in the specialized occupational fields of their agencies—but not as managers per se, for few have been trained for management;

most of those designated as staff are also professionals, but typically in fields of specialism different from that of management;

many of the workers—and most of those in middle-management positions—are also professionals, usually in the same professions as management.

Commonly there is a mutually supportive relationship between the professional managers and the professional workers in the same profession. The former see themselves, and are viewed by the latter, as representative of the interests of both.

Further, there may be no conflict between the organization and its objectives on the one hand and the aspirations and standards of its professional workers and executives on the other. In a good many cases, the goals and standards of public agencies, as seen by their officers and employees, are identical with the goals and standards of the professions as they are seen by their members. This is true of most public organizations in fields such as public health, welfare, geology, forestry, education, and military affairs. The public organizations, the bureaucracies, not only heavily influence but actually determine and epitomize the goals of the professions which provide the leaders and many of the workers under them. In other words, the bureaucracies, with their official powers, funds, and activities, and the elite professions which people and often dominate bureaucracies with their educational backgrounds, cultures, standards, and prestige are mutually supportive and have common objectives.[8]

A more useful model of most sizable public organizations in government—at the department level and below in state and local units and at the bureau or service level and below in the federal government—would be one which recognized the internal professional and other vocational groupings and the stratification of these within each agency in terms of both prestige and power. In most public agencies which have been in operation for some time, there is a single occupational group whose knowledge, skills, and orientations are closely identified with the mission and activities of the agency. If the work is seen as requiring intellectual capacity and background education to the level of college graduation—and as we have seen, this is the case in an increasing majority of agencies—the group comes to constitute a professional elite. It is a *corps*—a body of men and women closely associated

---

8. Most of the relevant literature has emphasized the opposition of the professions and their values to organizations and their values, laying stress upon the demands of individual professionals for autonomy against organizational demands for group or social goals. It has ignored the frequent affinity between professions and the organizations which they govern and the organizational efforts, in many cases, to protect the professional autonomy of employees.

with each other and with the enterprise—and it is sometimes so designated. It is also a *core*: it is at the center of the agency, controls the key line positions, and provides the main, perhaps the exclusive, source of its leadership. If at the time the elite developed there was no existing profession clearly identified with the activities of the agency, it is likely to be a unique *public service profession*—military, Foreign Service, or public health, for example. If on the other hand there was a clearly related, existing, outside profession or if one subsequently developed, the elite may consist of members of a *general profession*—such as civil engineers in highway departments, psychiatrists in mental hygiene institutions, and lawyers in departments of justice. In some cases, the clearly different nature of the work of the public agencies has occasioned a split-off from an established profession and the birth of a new public service profession, which, however, has retained the educational base of the older one—as in the case of public health doctors and the emerging professions of public works engineers and educational administrators.

There are five principal types of exceptions to the professional elite structure. One is found in relatively new agencies where no existing profession can yet make a clear claim to status as the appropriate elite. A second exception occurs in agencies of the business type, such as the Postal Service and some publicly owned utilities, where the trichotomy of management, staff, and workers may be more descriptive. (In many utility operations, however, line management consists of professional engineers.) A third exception is found in those public agencies whose work does not, or does not yet, require higher education to the graduating level. Police and fire protection are examples of this, though both are moving in the direction of professionalization. Fourth are agencies which are controversial, unstable or temporary, or which, for political reasons, must avoid the appearance of permanence. Professional elitism entails a career orientation. (The Agency for International Development is a good current example in which the development of a technical assistance elite has been politically inhibited.) Finally, a few agencies were deliberately designed in such a way as to prevent dominance by a single occupation through their multipurpose missions. An historic example is the Tennessee Valley Authority, but interdisciplinary research laboratories offer abundant illustrations.

Professional elites in larger agencies tend to specialize into subdivisions under the general professional canopy. These may be reflections of well-recognized divisions of the profession, determined outside the agency and extending back into educational specialization, as in medicine and engineering. They may be grounded in specializations of work in the agency itself, sometimes highly formalized as in various arms and services of the Army (Engineer, Quartermaster, Infantry, Ordnance). Or they may be based upon continuing kinds of work assignments not formally recognized as separate corps or segments—e.g., the distinctions among personnel officers in activities such as recruiting, examining, classification, labor relations. Among such subgroups there is normally a pecking order of prestige and influence. The most elite of them is likely to be the one which historically was most closely identified with the end purpose, the basic content of the agency— the officers of the line in the Navy, the pilots in the Air Force, the political officers in the Foreign Service, the civil engineers in a construction agency which also employs electrical and mechanical engineers.

No organization of substantial size can consist solely of members of one occupation. There must always be supportive activities, carried on by individuals who are not members of the elite profession. Indeed, the number in the professional elite may constitute only a small minority of all employees; e.g., public health doctors in a local health office, psychiatrists in mental health institutions, social workers in welfare offices. Complex government agencies employ sizable numbers of professionals, specialists, and workers in fields other than the elite one. These may be grouped in the following main categories:

Supporting Line Professions: professionals who carry on and contribute to the substantive work of the agency, but are trained and experienced in different fields. Thus in a state mental health department and in state mental institutions the psychiatrists are the elite, but by far the greater numbers are psychologists, psychiatric nurses, and social workers. A forestry operation includes agronomists, botanists, engineers, and many others.

Staff Professions: advisers and technicians for their specialized knowledge in areas related to, but not central to, the line work of the agency—as economists, sociologists, legal counsel, design engineers, computer analysts in many kinds of agencies. These are usually few in number and relatively high in grade and position, though not at the very top.

Administrative Professions: officials engaged in personnel, budget, finance, communications, purchasing, supply. Some of these can be found in almost every large agency, although in some the positions are filled by members of the elite professions, particularly at the level of leadership. Most of these are "emergent" rather than established professions.

Workers: paraprofessionals, supervisors, clerical, service, skilled, and unskilled personnel.

Figure 1 is a "still picture" of the composition of a hypothetical public agency, well-established and operating in a professional field. (Hypothetical examples of the schema in particular kinds of agencies are shown in Table 2.) The vertical dimension is organizational rank or level of pay, and may be assumed to equate very roughly with the level of day-to-day responsibility of incumbents. The horizontal dimension represents the numbers of persons at each grade. The horizontal lines at the bottom of the figures represent the normal and the sometimes exclusive entering-level of beginners when they are appointed in the various categories. The horizontal lines and points at the top of the various figures represent the

Figure 1. Schematic Diagram of Composition of a
Professionalized Government Agency

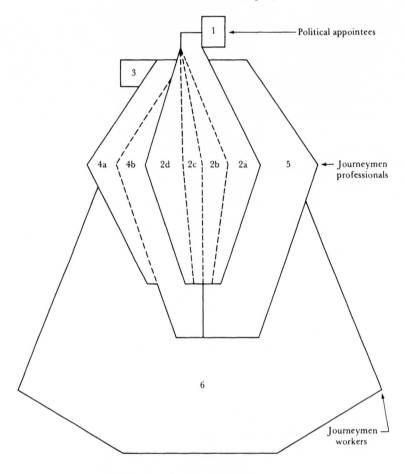

KEY: 1. Political appointees from outside the agency
2. The elite profession:
   2a. The elite segment of the elite profession
   2b, c, d. Other segments of the elite profession
3. Staff professions
4. Line professions
5. Administrative professions
6. Workers, including supervisors, paraprofessionals, clerical, manual,
   and others

highest grade an individual in each category can expect to reach. For an employee to cross lines from one category to another is usually difficult and, where professional standards are high and clear-cut, may be impossible, even illegal. The diamond shapes of the elite profession (2) and of the other professional groups (4 and 5) are typical of most such groups in government where professionals are hired soon after completing their education on a junior basis and advance rapidly to journeyman-level work. The trapezoidal (as distinguished from the familiar pyramidal) shape of the organization as a whole is also representative, although in most agencies the percentage of the total who are professional personnel is much smaller than is represented on the chart. Over the course of time, the normal progress of an employee in any category is upward, but obviously only a few will make it all the way to the top.

At the top of the diagram are represented a small number of political appointees, recruited from outside, who may or may not be professional. With these are included some poltical appointees drawn from the elite segment of the elite profession. Most of the very top career jobs are also filled from this group, and almost all of such jobs are filled by the elite profession. The incumbents of these jobs constitute very roughly what Morris Janowitz has described as the "elite nucleus."[9]

The diagram suggests that those who make it to the very top, the "elite of the elite," have pursued a more or less orthodox and "proper" type of career. The implication appears to be erroneous in some cases and may indeed be widely untrue. Janowitz found a substantial proportion of the military elite nucleus to be individuals who had pursued unorthodox, innovative careers. A study of the U.S. Foreign Service some years ago indicated that among the Foreign

9. *The Professional Soldier: A Social and Political Portrait* (Glencoe, Ill., The Free Press, 1964), Chapter 8.

Table 2. Illustrative but Hypothetical Examples
of Social Organizations of Public Agencies

	Department of State	*Department of Air Force*
1. Political Appointees	Secy.; Under-secys. and some Asst. Secys.	Secretary, Under-secys. and Asst. Secys.
2. Elite Profession	FSO's	Air Force Officers
2a. elite segment	Political Officers	Flying "
2b. other "	Economic "	Logistics "
2c. other "	Consular "	Maintenance"
2d. other "	Administrative Officers	Administrative Officers
3. Staff Professions	Legal Advisers Scientific Advisers Public Relations Officers	General Counsel Scientific Advisers Public Information Officers
4. Line Professions	a. Reserve Officers (various fields) b. Civil Service (various fields)	Reserve Officers (various fields) Civil Service (various fields)
5. Administrative Professions	Officers in Finance, Budget, Personnel, Training, Supply, Communications, Purchasing, etc. (Civil Service and F.S. Staff Officers)	(Civil Service and Noncom. Enlisted)
6. Nonprofessional Employees	Sub-Professional, Clerical, Labor, Custodial, etc. (Civil Service and F.S. Staff)	(Civil Service and Enlisted)

State Department of Highways	State Department of Mental Health	Local Department of Health
Department Head and Deputies	Department Head and Deputies	Department Head
Engineers Civil Engineers Electrical " Mechanical " Industrial "	M.D.s Psychiatrists Surgeons Pathologists	M.D.s Public Health M.D.s Pediatricians

Counsel
Economists
Public Relations
  Officers
Real Estate
  Appraisers
	Counsel
	Sociologists
	Statisticians
		Counsel
		Sociologists
		Bio-statisticians

Scientists—Civil
  Service (various
  fields)
Technicians—Civil
  Service (various
  fields)
	Clinical Psychologists
	Psychiatric Social
	  Workers
	Psychiatric Nurses
		Sanitary Engineers
		Public Health
		  Nurses
		Social Workers

⟶	⟶	⟶
(Civil Service)	(Civil Service)	(Civil Service)
⟶	⟶	⟶
(Civil Service)	(Civil Service)	(Civil Service)

Service Officers in executive positions in Washington and overseas, a disproportionate number had entered the service laterally (i.e., unorthodoxly).[10] Whether these findings about the top leadership in the Foreign Service and the military are typical of professionalized public agencies or arise from certain special circumstances is a significant though largely unexplored question.

Note that the arrangement of professional elites within different agencies does not necessarily reflect the status and prestige of the different professions in the society at large, nor does it reflect the amount of education beyond the bachelor's degree. The determining element is the historic and current identification of the specialty with the central content and purpose of the agency's work. Registered nurses are the elite of a visiting nurse association but not of a hospital. Engineers are the elite of a state highway department but not of a scientific laboratory. Masters of social work are elite in a welfare department but not in a mental hospital. Psychiatrists are the elite profession (or a segment if medical doctors are considered a single profession) in a mental hospital but not in a general hospital or in a local, state, or national public health office. Scientists are the elite in a scientific laboratory, but not in a U.S. embassy overseas.

Note also that within large departments there may be a number of different systems of elitism at different levels in the organization. Professionals in a given field tend to form an associational community which is often the basis for formal organizational differentiation. To a considerable extent, therefore, the suborganization of many departments conforms to professional definitions. Within each major unit there is a professional elite, which may not be the same as the elite of the larger organization. Thus architects are likely to

10. John E. Harr, *The Anatomy of the Foreign Service: A Statistical Profile* (New York, Carnegie Endowment for International Peace, Foreign Affairs Study No. 4, 1965), Chapter VI.

be the elite *within* an architectural division which includes many engineers among other professionals; but if the division is a part of a department of public works, the architects yield in elite status to the civil engineers at the departmental level. Similarly, geologists are the elite in the U.S. Geological Survey but not in the Department of Interior.

Thirdly, it may be noted that the elite status of professions in many different public agencies is relatively but not completely stable. The knowledge, technique, and orientation of the older professions tend toward obsolescence in the face of growing science, new kinds of problems, and new understandings about how to deal with them. These tendencies cast the older professional elites in a stance that is defensive and conservative vis-à-vis their positions and their control over agency objectives and programs. The intra-agency structure of elitism is, in many organizations, a battleground between a professional elite, or an elite segment, and other professions, other segments, and nonprofessionals. Political leaders desirous of rapid development of new programs may, and frequently do, endeavor to tip the balance against the elite professionals by appointing or selecting for promotion individuals who represent points of view at variance with the elite.

The key zones of potential tension and conflict in agencies of this kind lie not between management and workers, though these are not absent; nor between management and professionals, because most of the managers are themselves professional; nor between professionals and workers as such, since many of the workers are professionals. Rather they are delineated by the vertical lines (solid and dotted) in Figure 1. Specifically, they include tensions between:

1. politically appointed officials and the elite profession (or its elite segment), especially if the political leaders are not members of the profession (or segment);
2. different and competing segments of the elite profession;
3. the elite profession (or elite segment) and other professions in

the agency, including especially those in line and administrative professions.

My unproven observation is that the most conflictive situations in professionalized but not unionized public agencies arise between those in different professions (or segments) and in different personnel systems who are approximately equal in level of responsibility and pay, but where one is "more elite" than the other. That is, the principal tensions are horizontal and diagonal rather than vertical. Personnel who are clearly subordinate are more likely to look upon their professional superiors as defenders and representatives than as competitors or opponents; and the professional superiors regard their own role in the same somewhat paternalistic fashion. This is less true in programs staffed by unionized employees, and with the growing organization of public employees it has changed substantially in the recent past. Still, a professional's status is not threatened by his or her secretary, bookkeeper, or janitor. The professional can, and often does, "go to bat" for them, and they may look upon him or her as their principal advocate. Not so professionals in other segments and professions who are free to challenge the other's competence or judgment.

Each profession brings to an organization its own particularized view of the world and of the agency's role and mission in it. The perspective and motivation of each professional are shaped, at least to some extent, by the lens provided by professional education, prior professional experience, and professional colleagues. These distinctive views are further molded and strengthened through training and experience in the agency itself; and where the professional corps within the agency is one of long standing, where it operates through a well-entrenched career system, and where there is a vigorously defended stratification between the professional elite and others in the organization, these post-entry forces can be very strong indeed.

The analysis of different public organizations in terms of

their professional structure and intraprofessional and inter-professional systems of relationships is basic to a true understanding of how they work. Important decisions are likely to be the product of intraprofessional deliberation, representing the group views of the elite profession in the agency, compromised in some cases to satisfy the demands of other professions and nonprofessionals. Social relationships outside the office usually parallel professional relationships within. Members of the same profession in an agency are "colleagues," like professors in a university; and the flavor of their work is similarly collegial. Toward members of other professions, their behavior is likely to be more formal, sometimes suspicious or even hostile. Toward paraprofessionals and other workers, the relationship may more frequently be paternalistic, patronizing, or dictatorial. Members of the elite profession identify their own work and that of the agency with their profession; the others are a little "outside," they are supplementary or supporting. The "climate" of an organization as well as its view of mission and its effectiveness in carrying it out are in considerable part a product of its professional structure and professional value system.

The Public Employment of Professionals

As the professional composition of public agencies has substantially revolutionized their internal anatomy, physiology, and nervous systems, so has the emergence of professions revolutionized the precepts and practices of public employment. Both revolutions continue with the development and solidification of new fields and new subspecialties. Although there are large differences in precepts and practices among different jurisdictions of government, the basic directions in public service employment are clear. They also are probably inevitable. They apply to virtually all professional fields, whether or not under civil service laws. They are often at odds with the most central—and most cherished—principles associated with civil service reform in this country: equal opportunity to apply and compete for jobs; competitive examinations for selection and (sometimes) promotion; equal pay for equal work; neutral and objective direction and control of the personnel system.

The most important of the changes is the last one, which involves the direction of personnel activities; it underlies the others. In general, what has happened (and is happening) is a *delegation* of real personnel authority, formal and/or informal, from a central personnel office or civil service commission to the professions and the professionals themselves.[11]

A basic drive of every profession, established or emergent, is *self-government* in deciding policies, criteria, and standards for employment and advancement, and in deciding individual personnel matters. The underlying argument for such professional hegemony is that no one outside—no amateur—is equipped to judge or even to understand the true content of the profession or the ingredients of merit in its practice. This thesis is difficult to challenge, particularly in highly developed, specialized, and scientized fields with which an amateur—or a professional in personnel administration—can have only a passing acquaintance.

The means whereby the professionals assert their control over personnel policies and actions are many and diverse. Some are specified and required by law or regulation; others grow out of gentlemen's agreements within—or in spite of—civil service laws; some reflect a silent abdication by the civil service agencies or a failure to assume an effective role; and some are unintended (or mayhap intended) consequences of others. I shall discuss them under three headings: influence and control by the professional elites within governmental

11. The word "delegation" is not precisely accurate in a good many fields, since many developed independently of any central personnel office, and there was no real *process* of delegation. But delegation is a reasonably accurate description of the product, whatever the nature of the evolution which preceded it.

agencies; influence and control by "outside" professions and their organizations; and influence and control by institutions of professional education.

Professional Elites. The extreme examples of professional control within agencies are provided by the various commissioned corps in the federal government which have never been under a general civil service system. Here one finds the most consolidated mechanisms of internal control by the elite group and particularly by senior members—the *elite cadre,* as Janowitz termed it. They determine the standards and criteria for entrance; the policies and procedures of assignment; the appropriate work content of elite corps positions; the criteria for promotion. They also set up the machinery for personnel operations, usually including boards, all or a majority of whose members are drawn from the corps itself. They also superintend the policies and operations of personnel management for other employees, including other professionals, who are not in the elite, yielding as little as they must to civil service requirements, to other employee groups, to outside professional interests, and to political pressures.

Much of this personnel control is sanctioned by law. It is significant that personnel matters in the various corps carry such preeminent weight and importance. Historically in the Army the handling of personnel was long entrusted to the staff division known as G-1 (A-1 in the Air Force); today the officers in charge of personnel are first deputy chiefs of staff. In the State Department the Board of Foreign Service has, since its founding, been essentially a personnel board, as the Director General of the Foreign Service has been primarily concerned with matters of personnel. It may be noted too that in these cases the professional elites have assumed control over the administration of agency personnel who are not in the corps: reserve officers, enlisted personnel (or Foreign Service staff), and civil servants.

Among the agencies not dominated by a commissioned

corps, professional control over personnel matters has been less conspicuous but still effective. In many cases it is carried out under the canopy of civil service laws and regulations. The professional elites normally have the most influential voice in determining personnel policies, standards, and criteria within broad prescriptions of civil service law. The recent trend toward decentralization, both at the federal level and in other large jurisdictions, has of course facilitated this development. Personnel selection for professionals is in many places left to boards, which are usually dominated by agency professionals. As will be seen later, competitive written and performance examinations in most of the established professional fields have largely been abandoned in favor of evidences of qualification determined outside the agency and indeed outside the civil service system. What is left—normally an "unassembled" examination of the candidates' records and/or an oral examination—is conducted by boards composed principally of members of the agency's elite profession. The same situation pertains to other personnel actions: assignments, promotions, disciplinary actions. In most cases the central influence is that of the agency; and if it is controlled by a professional elite, the basic control lies with that elite. The civil service or personnel agency provides assistance in recruitment, a certain amount of professional personnel guidance, certain procedural requisites, and participation and perhaps inspection to ensure conformance with regulations. The substance of personnel policy and decision rests, however, in the professional elite.

Our studies conducted some years ago of employment practices of federal, state, and local jurisdictions in California in general confirmed the tendency toward professional elite control of policies, standards, and actions within the agencies in which there was a professional elite. There were, of course, variations in the degree of control and in the techniques whereby it was made effective. In general, these variations seemed responsive to two factors: first, the degree to which the professional group had established itself as truly elite within a given agency; and second, the degree to which demand exceeded supply for professionals in the field in question. The better established, more recognized professions had greater control, as did those in which supply was scarcest. In our California studies, we found this to be true at all levels of government in the employment of lawyers, natural scientists, engineers, doctors, social workers, and health professionals. In the federal government, we found it true also for foresters, architects, and some others. In the state of California, it applied to psychiatrists in mental hygiene; among local governments, it applied in varying degrees to recreation workers, city planners, librarians, and some others.

The Professionals and Their Organizations. Among the established general professions, the practice of licensing practitioners is an old one. Indeed, it is a common index of whether or not a profession is truly "established," and many of the aspiring newer fields are seeking it to give them official and legal sanction. The licensing of professionals, as of craftsment, is normally accomplished by the legal delegation of state powers to a board, itself composed exclusively or predominantly of members of the profession. It normally requires the passing of an examination, drafted and graded by the board or other professional group. In all of this, the public personnel organization usually plays no part, and the examinations themselves are directed almost exclusively to the knowledge and skills required for private practice, not to governmental policy and managerial problems, nor to those of large organizations of any kind. In well-established fields, such as law, medicine, dentistry, architecture, some kinds of engineering, and school teaching, licensing is normally requisite to practice at the journeyman level. In others, it is essential to advancement to higher levels of responsibility and supervision: accounting and nursing, for example.

Governmental agencies, other than the licensing boards

themselves, play little part in the licensing process and have little influence upon or even interest in the content and standards of the examinations. Very probably, the finding of James W. Fesler in his 1942 study *The Independence of State Regulatory Agencies* is still accurate: "Professional licensing boards are virtually the creatures of the professional societies. . . ."[12] Yet it is clear that these examinations significantly affect the education and the qualifications which make for a professional man or woman. The governments by and large accept those qualifications as gospel in their own employment. In some fields (e.g., law, medicine) a license is an absolute requisite to employment at any professional level. In others, while not required, it may be sufficient evidence for hiring—without further evidence of qualification—and a basis for preferential treatment for advancement as well. Professionals who have gained their credentials in most fields are likely to escape any further tests of competence and knowledge if they aspire to enter government employ. For them the governments have abandoned to the professions the testing of merit insofar as it can be determined by examinations of knowledge and skill. Further, the licensing tests are noncompetitive among the candidates. Qualifications are measured only in terms of passing a minimum standard—which may of course be a high one.

But perhaps most important is the effect of the licensing structure upon the content, the dimensions, and the boundaries of the individual professions. As Corinne Lathrop Gilb has observed: "Public administrators generally fail to acknowledge *the extent to which the structure and composition of regulatory boards affect the division of labor and authority in the work world.*"[13] And the "work world" of course includes the administration of government itself.

12. Chicago, Public Administration Service, pp. 60–61.
13. *Hidden Hierarchies: The Professions and Government* (New York, Harper & Row, 1966), p. 194. (Author's emphasis.)

Professional Education. Over the long pull, the most profound impact upon the professional public services is that of the universities—their professional schools, their departments in the physical and social sciences which produce professionals, and their faculties in general. Higher education produces the bulk of future professionals. By their images, and by their impressions upon students, the schools have a great influence upon who opts for what fields and what kinds of young people—of what quality, what interests, what values —go where. It is clear too that they influence the choices by students among employers—whether government or other, and which jurisdictions and agencies of government. By their curricula, their faculties, their teaching, they define the content of each different specialism and the expectations and aspirations of the students in each. These students will of course include the principal operators in government tomorrow and the principal leaders the day after tomorrow.

In most professional fields, governments have accepted, without much question or knowledge, the academic definition of content and the academic criteria of qualification and merit. Most governments, like other employers, rely heavily upon credentials; possession of the sheepskin from an accredited institution is enough. Accreditation itself is normally based upon a review and approval of a given school's program by a committee of a larger organization composed of, or dominated by, professional educators in the same field. It reflects a consensus among academics as to the minimal curricular and faculty requirements necessary to produce qualified practitioners. In some fields accreditation and high academic standing (grade point average) are more important to governmental employers than professional licenses. In fields for which licensing has been provided in only a few states (or in none)—like social work, city planning, or librarianship—accreditation and grades become almost the sole criteria. Accreditation moreover is sometimes a requirement for licensing. Where government employers have any significant choice among candidates for jobs in the recognized professions, their reliance is placed upon 1. whether they come from accredited schools, 2. their grade point averages, and 3. the recommendations of professors. All three are of course academic determinants.

In the main, governments have yielded to the universities and professional educators the significant influences, the criteria, and the choices about public employment. Few of our larger governmental units give any competitive examinations on substance—that is, knowledge and skill—for candidates in professional fields. They leave it largely to the universities to determine what knowledges and skills are appropriate, and who among the graduating students are deserving of appointment. In a few fields, they also rely upon licensing examinations, themselves controlled by practitioners and educators outside of government. Among the agencies dominated by an elite professional corps, personnel decisions are largely dictated by the corps.

It is interesting that the Congress reaffirmed in the Veterans' Preference Act of 1944 its long-standing suspicion of formal academic qualifications for civil service jobs:

> No minimum educational requirement will be prescribed in any civil service examination except for such scientific, technical, or professional positions the duties of which the Civil Service Commission decides cannot be performed by a person who does not have such education.[14]

The Civil Service Commission (now the Office of Personnel Management) has since excepted virtually all of the estab-

14. The wording but not the sense of this provision was subsequently modified. See 80 Stat. 89-554, Sept. 6, 1966, p. 419. For an overview and explanation of the rationale for the exception of particular professions from the prohibition against minimum educational requirements see U.S. Office of Personnel Management, *Qualification Standards for Positions under the General Schedule*: Handbook X-118, (Washington, D.C., Government Printing Office, January 1979).

lished and general professional fields, a great many emergent professions including some that are exclusive to government, and a majority of the natural, life, and social scientists. The omissions from the civil service exceptions are more conspicuous than the exceptions themselves. Attorneys are of course omitted since they are not in the classified service anyway. Officials in administrative fields, such as budgeteers, personnel specialists, purchasing officers, tax administrators, and administrative officers are not excepted. None of the fields normally considered among the humanities at universities is excepted; and among social scientists, the political scientists, public administrators, and historians are conspicuous in not being excepted from the Congressional fiat. Anthropologists, economists, psychologists, and sociologists are all excepted.

The professional suspicion and opposition toward politics and government, suggested earlier, are probably even more vigorous among university professors. Here they are strengthened by the creeds of academic freedom and professorial autonomy. Apparently, the further one progresses through higher education, the less he or she is enticed by governmental employment; and this must reflect to some extent the influence of university faculties.[15]

In this chapter we have come full circle. Near the beginning, I discussed the impact of the knowledge explosion upon our society; near the end, I discussed the impact of the universities upon public employment. The latter is a facet of the former. As knowledge has grown and as occupations have been increasingly professionalized, the public services have become more dependent upon the founts of knowledge, the universities. In their own organizations, governments have

15. On this point, see especially Franklin P. Kilpatrick, Milton C. Cummings, Jr., and M. Kent Jennings, *The Image of the Federal Service* and the accompanying *Source Book* (Washington, D.C., The Brookings Institution, 1964).

both reflected and influenced the occupational structure of the society. In so doing they have benefited tremendously through the advancement in the level of knowledge and skill in every field. They may also have suffered in the degree to which the central governments could control and direct operations in the general interest. For in the process, they have yielded a great deal of influence over *who* will conduct and direct individual programs, and how the content of programs will be defined as well.

For better or worse—or better *and* worse—much of our government is now in the hands of professionals (including scientists). The choice of these professionals, the determination of their skills, and the content of their work are now principally determined, not by general governmental agencies, but by their own professional elites, professional organizations, and the institutions and faculties of higher education. It is unlikely that the trend toward professionalism in or outside of government will soon be reversed. But the educational process through which the professionals are produced and later refreshed (in continuing educational programs) can be restudied and conceivably changed. The need for broadening, for humanizing, and in some fields for lengthening professional education programs may in the long run prove more crucial to governmental response to societal problems than any amount of civil service reform.

6

Three Systems of Merit

Much of the literature about public personnel lays such heavy emphasis upon the civil service and civil service reform that one may be led to the mistaken impression that the public service consists of two elements: those employed under civil service laws and rules (the good guys) and the politicians (the bad guys). My own stress upon the evolution of a neutral civil service in Chapters 3 and 4 is similarly skewed, for it quite ignores the development of other parts of the public service which are neither political nor civil service in the traditional sense. These other parts comprise nearly half of all public employment and include part or all of three of its biggest sectors: military personnel, school teachers, and skilled and unskilled labor.

It may be well at the outset to frame the entire topic in statistical terms.[1] In 1980, nearly one of every five working

---

1. Most of the data in this and the following paragraph are drawn from the *Budget of the United States Government, Fiscal Year 1982, Special Analyses* (Washington, D.C., U.S. Government Printing Office, 1981) Table I-2, p. 282, and Table I-5, p. 288. Data for the earlier years are drawn from the Bureau of the Census, *Historical Statistics of the United States* (Washington, D.C., U.S. Government Printing Office, 1975), p. 1141. For the breakdowns on categories of occupations I have relied upon Bureau of Labor Statistics, "The 1978 Class of Worker Matrix for the United States," an unpublished and undated table.

Americans worked directly for a government, federal, state or local. About one eighth of these, roughly 2 percent of the employed labor force, were officers or enlisted personnel in the military service. More than four fifths of all civilian employees in government worked at state and local levels, not federal, and of these about one quarter were teachers. The crafts and skilled and unskilled labor accounted for about 15 percent of governmental personnel, and a good many of these were not employed in the traditional civil service fashion.

In this connection, the historic trends of public employment may be of some interest, partly because they provide some clues to the future, partly because many popular impressions are so wide of the mark. Over the past thirty years, federal civilian employment has been nearly static—and even downward when measured against the U.S. population it is intended to serve. In 1952, there were 16.3 federal civilians per 1000 of population; in 1980, the comparable proportion was 12.5. (Both figures include the postal workers.) There has been a sharp decline in military personnel since the end of the Vietnam War and the replacement of the draft with the all-volunteer force. In relation to total population, all federal civilian and military employment combined grew from 25 per 1000 in 1947, to 31 in 1957, to 32 in 1967. Since then, following some growth during the Vietnam period, there has been a fairly steady and persistent decline to 22 per 1000 in 1980—lower than the figure for 1947. On the other hand, state and local employment has risen rapidly and consistently since the early 1950s but seems now to be leveling off. In 1952, 38.4 percent of all civilian employees in American government were federal; by 1980, the comparable proportion was less than half that: 17.3 percent. The biggest increases among the functions of government have occurred in education and health, and most of the employees in these fields are of course in state and local governments.

So it behooves us, if we are to gain a balanced picture of

the whole public service, to look beyond the civil service type of system—as well as the patronage type of system—since both together comprehend not much more than half of public personnel. The framing of a satisfactory typology of personnel systems, however, is a challenge. In the first place, American governments have displayed almost unbelievable ingenuity in developing different kinds of arrangements for the employment of personal services, ranging from compulsion (selective service) to volunteers (Peace Corps, .Vista, and others), to volunteers without compensation (WOC), and employees of government contractors, with a great variety of categories in between. Another difficulty arises from the distance one finds between law and regulation on the one hand and attitude and practice on the other. There are substantial numbers of departments and agencies in state, county, district, and city governments which are under no legal civil service but still employ people in accordance with orthodox civil service practices. Conversely, there are departments and agencies at all levels of government which are legally under civil service whose employment practices bear little relationship to the traditional merit system.

For purposes of description, analysis, and comparison, it is useful to classify the public services into four main types of personnel systems:

1. *political appointees*: without tenure;
2. *general civil service*: white-collar personnel, mostly nonprofessional, who enjoy tenure, de jure, de facto or both, and whose employment is administered in accordance with traditional civil service practices with emphasis upon *the position*;
3. *career system*: white-collar personnel, mostly professional or paraprofessional, who enjoy tenure in agency and occupation though not in positions, and whose employment is administered as a progressive, preferably planned development with emphasis upon *the person* rather than the position;
4. *collective system*: blue-collar plus an increasing proportion of

white-collar personnel (from categories 2 and 3 above), whose
employment is governed primarily or in substantial part
through bargaining between union or association and governmental jurisdiction.

This grouping does not by any means comprehend all those
people who make up the public service or all the methods
whereby public servants are employed, but it does include
most of those in executive branches who have continuing impact upon public policy. The boundaries around each category are not clear-cut, and they are moving. There are gray
areas between one and another, particularly between the
political on the one hand and both the general service and
the career system on the other, and between the general service and the career system. There is unquestionably a tendency of movement from the general service toward the
career service as high-level occupational specialisms develop
standards, coalesce, and become recognized—that is, as they
become professional. There has also been a growing movement from the general service and the career systems in the
direction of the collective category as labor organization has
become stronger among both general civil service and professional workers.

In the descriptions and analyses that follow the four categories are treated, for purposes of clarity and emphasis, as
extremes or, in Weberian terminology, as "ideal types." Yet
none is "ideal," at least in terms of my system of values, and
none, as presented, is "typical." The distinctions, if overdrawn, are nevertheless clear and important. Each category
has a different role, function, and influence in the larger governmental system; each operates under a different set of constraints and according to a different set of loyalties and iden-
tifications; and each is employed by governments according
to its own set of proprieties and expectations. All are, or can
be, "merit systems" if one accepts a liberal definition of the
term. But the criteria of merit in the various categories differ
widely in accordance with their role and mission in the

polity. Each presents its own distinctive complex of problems for democracy.

It should be observed that the division of the public service into four categories does not by any means correspond with organizational differentiation. Most sizable public organizations include at least three categories (general service, career system, and blue-collar workers), and many include all four. This means, among other things, that for most public agencies there must be at least three different systems of personnel administration, even though all may be covered within the same set of laws and rules.

It should also be noted that the four categories do not represent vertical class distinctions, corresponding to and reenforcing a four-class society, even though, by and large, the political officers probably enjoy the highest prestige and hierarchical power and the collective groups are probably the lowest in prestige though often well up the scale in terms of financial reward. Many in all the first three categories are educated at or beyond the college level, and all four participate in decisions, though in different ways and on different subjects. It is interesting to contrast this classification with that applicable to the public services in Europe, which clearly derives from social class divisions, operating through the intermediacy of the educational system (see Chapter 2).

The remainder of this chapter concerns the first three categories listed on p. 145. The general civil service and the career systems are juxtaposed for purposes of contrast, and a discussion of political appointments follows. The fourth category, the collective system, presents certain special problems for a democratic state and is considered separately in the following chapter.

Career Systems and the General Civil Service

Both the career systems and the general civil service system of public employment developed in this country partly in reaction *against* the political spoils system. Both are thought of as merit systems; indeed, members of career systems often view incursions of general civil service practices into their territory as violations of merit. On the other hand, the general civil service itself is often referred to as a career service, especially to contrast it with political appointments. Yet, historically and ideologically, the career system and the general service are a long distance apart. The two seem to be moving toward one another, as I shall show later, although their differences in operations and in consequences remain significant and often vivid.

The origins and development of the general civil service system and the characteristics which derived from this history were discussed in Chapters 3 and 4. Career systems have two origins, one ancient, the other relatively recent. The model of the old career system—the "ideal type"—is that of the military officers of the Army, Navy, Air Force, and Marines. The most nearly "ideal" of the ideal type today is probably the personnel system of the officers of the line in the U.S. Navy. The military system has been copied in or adapted to a number of other federal activities—in fact, virtually all which employ commissioned officers: the Foreign Service, the Public Health Service, the Coast Guard. It has also been, in varying degree, a model for state and local police systems and for local fire departments, although in a good many of these it collided with the egalitarian philosophies of spoils and the civil service systems, and was severely modified.

The underlying concepts of these older career systems, especially the military and the diplomatic, are rooted in distant history, long before the founding of the United States and at least as far back as European feudalism. Some sociologists have attributed the basic distinction between military officers and enlisted men to the feudal class distinctions between lords and vassals during the feudal era. As a matter of fact, it probably predates feudalism. Likewise the titles, prerogatives, and roles encompassed in the U.S. Foreign

Service can be traced in some part to the formal relations between the heads of states of many centuries ago. Associated with such age is a rich body of tradition and a deep feeling of attachment on the part of members of the service toward the service itself, a feeling that approaches veneration. It is hardly necessary to observe that such a feeling is quite unlike that of the typical general service employee toward the civil service. In the one case the personnel system is an *institution*; in the other it is merely a *means of employment*. Most of these older career services are identified with a single employing organization over which they have an historic near-monopoly of control. And in their self-image, they associate themselves with the service, not the organization, which they take for granted.

The difference in attitude is illustrated by one's response to a question as to what his or her occupation is. A non-professional civil servant working in the Department of the Navy is most likely to respond, "I work for the Navy Department"; an officer is more likely to say, "I am an officer in the Navy." Some years ago a questionnaire survey of Foreign Service officers asked this question: How would you respond if asked by a stranger at a party as to what your occupation is? Half replied, "I'm a Foreign Service Officer." Another third responded either, "I'm in the Foreign Service," or "I'm in the diplomatic service." Only one in eight said, "I work for the State Department."

The more recent style of career system has attended the development of individual professions—new professions in response, primarily to new kinds of governmental programs, or specialized subdivisions of general professions, or members of general professions which have well-developed professional career lines both in and out of government. The first of these types—new occupational fields which, at the time of their founding, were exclusively or predominantly employed by governmental agencies—are represented by various agricultural specialists, city managers, foresters, geologists, social workers, and city planners; the second—offshoots of established professions—by public health specialists in various fields, highway engineers, space scientists. The third includes professionals performing their trade in governmental employ, but according to the career standards and processes of the profession itself—doctors, dentists, lawyers, architects, etc. Most of these, as they grow and develop their own self-identification within government, tend toward career systems of employment, distinct from the main body of unprofessionalized civil service and from the other career services.

In spite of substantial differences among the various professional fields, there are certain common denominators of concept and practice similar to those of the older services, as exemplified by the various commissioned corps. These common denominators distinguish them from political appointees on the one hand and the general service on the other. In the paragraphs that follow are set forth the principal characteristics of career system ideology and practice which distinguish them from the traditional civil service under four headings: general attributes; operating characteristics in terms of personnel administration; consequences in terms of governmental decision-making, operations, and democratic control; and finally the challenges set by our evolving society.

General Attributes

The first attribute is really a definition. A career system is an employment system built upon a given specialization of preparation, knowledge, and skill for which one systematically prepares in one's junior years, which provides his or her first major job, and which assures him or her a progressive employment in that line of work until death or retirement. In a given jurisdiction of government the assurance traditionally lies within a single agency or department or a very few of them; but as parallel opportunities are established in other jurisdictions, careers may be pursued in comparable agencies in the same line of work.

A second attribute of career system is that there is a close identification between the system and the organization in which it operates. In fact, as suggested earlier, the personnel system supersedes the organization in the minds of the career servants. Elections and political leadership may come and go and organizational structures may be modified, but the career personnel system survives. It is easier to reorganize the Army than to bring about fundamental changes in the structure of the military personnel system.

This view was colorfully illustrated in a story (possibly apocryphal) attributed to Dwight Eisenhower when he was president of Columbia University. At a meeting with members of his faculty, Mr. Eisenhower alluded to professors as "employees of the University." A respected professor arose to correct him: "We are not employees of the University, Mr. President; we *are* the University." (In some ways academics are more nearly an "ideal type" of careerists than are the line officers of the Navy.) Professors, like others in career systems, prefer to think of themselves as "members" of a system—"faculty members"—rather than as "employees" of an organization.

There are two very significant corollaries to this identification of the career system with the organization and its objectives. One is the insistence on assignments of members of the system to the key line positions—that is, the positions with significant policy-making and decision-making authority. The members are pushed by this drive as high in the organization as is politically possible. This is of course precisely the same tendency we have already alluded to in connection with the professions. The second is the parallel drive to make the system self-governing as far as its personnel policies and decisions are concerned. Control of the criteria for entrance, for assignment, and for advancement and control of the application of those criteria is sought by accredited members of the system, quarantined as far as possible from outside (usually meaning political or amateur) interference. The same applies to other personnel matters; but in career systems especially, entrance, assignment, and advancement are the three key activities.

A third and related general attribute of career systems is the interdependence of the system and its members. Historically, the origin of most independent career systems may be traced to their monopoly character in the employment market. The Army was the only employer of Army officers, as were the Navy and the Foreign Service of their officers. This was largely true, in the beginning stages at least, of most of what are here called public service professions. Each profession required officials with particularized skills, abilities, and experience which could be gained only within the system itself. It may be noted that this is in direct contrast to the historic assumption of our civil service system that the schools and colleges and private employers could produce all the skills and knowledge required.

To a less pronounced extent, the same phenomenon has occurred in agencies dominated by members of general (as distinguished from public service) professions. The qualifications for entry were the same as, and therefore were competitive with, those of other employers. But if it were true, or if it could be claimed, that advancement to upper level positions required the kinds of experience that only *this* agency could provide, and if it could also be claimed that *this* kind of experience qualified career system members for no other kinds of employment, the monopoly character of the employment relationship would grow with the tenure of the members. This phenomenon contributes to a heightened feeling of interdependence between agency and member, which culminates in an actuality. The system would have invested a great deal of time, effort, and money in the recruitment of personnel and the new workers' development of journeymen and leadership status and could not afford to let them go in their prime. On the other side, every journeyman member of the system would have dedicated a good share of his or her working life to the development of capacities not of particular value to other employers. Each one—the system (or "organization") and its member—was dependent upon (or "stuck with") the other. This phenomenon probably contributed to the relatively more *paternalistic* personnel practices of career systems: their greater concern about progressive assignments, about employee welfare (including the welfare of employee families), about employee development and training programs, and about fringe benefits, including generous retirement benefits. Unlike most of the general service, a central problem of many of the career systems has been that turnover is *too low*, slowing advancement opportunities for the younger members. This has contributed to the lowering of retirement ages in these systems, and to the development of devices whereby those failing of advancement may be *selected* out; i.e., retired prematurely without prejudice or great financial sacrifice.

The potential dividends deriving from the close relationship between a career system and its members are very substantial. They include a relatively high sense of *loyalty* and *devotion* of the members to the system; and insofar as the system is identified with the organization and its purposes, to the latter also. There is a greater sense of *discipline* to behave in approved ways; to work according to the professional standards of the career system; and to accept assignments and tasks which are difficult, disagreeable, and sometimes hazardous. Insofar as one is confident that those in influential positions are associates with like orientations, experience, and ambitions, he or she is more likely to feel confident that his or her own destinies will be directed knowledgeably and fairly. Finally, there is a basis in communication and language, in orientation and experience, in long-standing association, for mutual understanding and sympathy among members of the system—a basis for *team spirit.*

The sense of "oneness" between a career system and its members has probably been strongest in those agencies for which there is only a single employer in the nation; that is, in the monopoly employers such as the military and the Foreign Service. But the same consequence occurs among many functional agencies in the states, cities, and counties where there is only one potential employer for a specialty at a given place and where most system members are unable or unwilling to move. In such situations there is a monopoly employment situation quite comparable to that of the military services.

There is however a great deal of evidence that the monopolistic character of career system employment in government is weakening. This is partly a consequence of the increasingly mutual interdependence and intrusion of the public and private sectors in the same problem areas. It is partly a consequence of increasing multi-national interests of private business; it is partly a consequence of interdependence of public-private organizations and of federal-state-local agencies. High-level experience in government in a great many fields has become a valuable qualification for high-level (and much better paying) positions in the private sector. A few years of government experience in a growing number of different occupational fields have become a persuasive qualification in the private sector. For example: law—as in regulation, taxation; medicine—as in research, psychiatry; forestry; procurement; foreign affairs (with particular reference to multinational corporations); physics; biological sciences; economics; to mention but a few.

These convergences—between national and international, between federal and state-local, between public and private, and among the various interconnected functional and specialized interests—are threatening to our accustomed educational and vocational habits. In a good many fields, the occupational and employment monopoly is dying, or has already been destroyed.

Fourth, there is in a career system a heavier emphasis upon, and recognition of, *status* than in the general service, an emphasis reflected not only in the various activities of personnel management but also in the behavior, interpersonal relationships, and attitudes of those in the organization. Status in a modern career system is based more upon *ascription* than upon *performance*; but it is ascribed not in consequence of family or social status, as in medieval societies, but of *initial achievement* in education, specialization, and conquest of the obstacles at the gates of entry. Increasingly it depends upon superior (or at least successful completion of) specialized education at a university, sometimes evidenced by passage of an accrediting examination, appointment, and successful completion of a probationary period. But once the young candidate has "made it" he or she is "in the career." If the individual is employed in an agency in which his or her field of specialism is dominant, he or she has acquired *status* above others in that organization who lack these credentials; and, with respect to the work and problems of that organization, has acquired status in the polity and the society in general. This is to say that in a career system ascribed status itself is achieved, not inherited, but once acquired depends rather less upon subsequent achievement than upon a basic and approved level of professional behavior and performance. Status gained in a given calling and organization is not automatically transferable to other kinds of activities and organizations and it is not necessarily equated with social status in society in general. A career system which is highly esteemed within an organization may indeed be little known or cared about in the outside world.

There is also heavier emphasis placed upon status *within* the career system itself to differentiate among its own members in a vertical pecking order. This is most pronounced and visible in the older career systems—the military where the symbols of rank are worn with the uniform, or the Foreign Service where rank determines seating arrangements at formal functions, among many other things. But it is true too of the newer ones: of the various ranks of engineers in a state highway department, of foresters in the U.S. Forest Service, of faculty members at a university. Rank, once acquired, is a more important determinant of prestige and sometimes of influence than are position, current responsibilities, and performance.

Another kind of internal status differentiation is that which elevates certain sub-specializations within the system itself. This is very pronounced and pervasive in some systems:

officers with wings in the Air Force

line officers of the Navy

Army officers of the Corps of Engineers; (there is a well recognized
  pecking order among the various arms and services of the Army)

political officers in the Foreign Service

civil engineers in a highway department

medical doctors in the U.S. Public Health Service.

Such status valuations among specializations are best known to the members of the systems themselves, and they have many subtle—as well as some not so subtle—effects upon behavior, operations, and decision making within organizations. Again, it may be observed that they may run directly counter to occupational prestige in the minds of the public. For example, lawyers in general probably have significantly higher public prestige than do engineers in general. But lawyers from the Office of the Judge Advocate General do not rank over engineers in the Army Corps of Engineers, nor flying officers in the Air Force, nor line officers in the Navy.

Personnel Operations

It is unnecessary here to specify in any detail the differences between the personnel practices of the general civil service and those of career systems: a broad-brush outline of the basic contrasts that characterize the approaches of the two types toward personnel decisions will suffice. Generalizing at this level is hazardous, for it invites a degree of exaggeration for purposes of emphasis; and the two kinds of systems are tending to become more alike, as will be demonstrated later. With this caveat in mind however, the differences between these "ideal types" are striking. Anyone who has observed two or more of them operating in the same organization—for example, civilian and officer personnel in any of the military services—will have recognized that a wide gulf separates them. This is the more surprising because personnel administration has to do in all public organizations with similar activities: recruiting and appointing new people, making assignments, developing skills, providing for promotions, handling separations, providing benefits, keeping records. But the wide spread in the kinds of emphases placed on these different activities, in the perspective from which they are approached, in the ways that they are done, makes it almost impossible to see that they are essentially the same things from one service to another. The following paragraphs emphasize those features of career systems which contrast most vividly with those of the general service.

The central conceptual difference lies in the career system's thesis that *rank inheres in the person* and depends upon the level of his or her advancement through a systematic and competitive promotion system, as against the general service thesis of *rank in the job*, determined by its difficulty and responsibility. This is the preeminently important difference because, from an operational standpoint, almost everything else flows from it. Position classification became in the general civil service the pivot of virtually all personnel activities; in the older career systems, it was virtually unknown until World War II, and it still has rather little influence in most of them.

Recruitment by the career systems was initially from a

rather select group of graduates from certain colleges (as in the Foreign Service) or nominees of Congressmen, usually from upper- and upper-middle-class families (as in the Army and Navy.) More recent professionalized career systems have required degrees from appropriate professional schools and passage of professional examinations by licensing boards in the states. The expectation of these systems has been that recruitment would be of young persons, upon completion of their education, for the bottom rung of the career ladder, which was still considerably above the bottom levels of the agency's employment. Leaders in career systems have always resisted *lateral entry* to career status at intermediate and upper grades. The general service on the other hand for many years deliberately avoided limitations upon applications due to age or formal education or level of job. Instead, it developed on an unspoken premise of an employer's market in which there would be qualified applicants for any type of vacancy.

The criterion of *selection* for career systems was and remains the potential of the candidate to develop in the system's line of work over his full career. In the general service, selection has traditionally been based on the candidates' promise to perform adequately in the job class which was immediately to be filled. It may be noted that both systems were and are competitive in fields in which there is an adequate supply of candidates, and both have departed from competitive methods where the supply is inadequate. But the underlying difference remains: one selects for a career, the other for a job. Further, career systems generally give more emphasis to, and are more rigorous about, probationary periods for new entrants to assure that new appointees are properly oriented, adjusted, and qualified to develop through the full career.

Advancement in career systems from junior to full journeyman status is largely automatic, provided the employee has successfully completed his or her probationary period and commits no negative or disqualifying acts thereafter. But promotions above the basic journeyman level are based upon a scheduled, person-to-person review in which each member competes with all others at the same level, and without regard to specific job vacancies (though within general budgetary limits). Candidates for promotion are protected from competition with outsiders, or at least so they hope. In the general service, advancements depend upon specific job vacancies at higher levels, are not restricted to one grade, may or may not be competitive, and are not protected against possible encroachment by outsiders. Career systems are much more careful and thorough in building systematic written records and evaluations of their members, primarily for decisions on promotions. Determinations about individual promotions are customarily made by boards consisting of equal and higher ranking members of the system, sometimes supplemented by a minority of outside members and subject to a variety of reviews and appeals. Promotion is a very important matter in career systems, not one to be left to a personnel office, a supervisor, or a competitive examination. Consequently the performance and the behavior of members of a career system are heavily conditioned by their expectations of the criteria the boards will apply in reviewing their candidacies.

Forward *personnel planning* has been more necessary and generally far more advanced in the career systems than in the general civil service, except in highly specialized areas where there was an obvious shortage of qualified personnel. This is true in two quite different dimensions: the *macro*-planning for the personnel of the system as a whole, and the *micro*-planning of the careers of individual members within the system. Systemwide planning for a good many years in the future is essential if the system restricts itself to entry at the bottom level. The nature and numbers of entries in the current year depend upon one's estimate of the needs for journeymen five to twenty-five years hence and of leadership personnel ten to forty years hence. Next year's budget and recruitment plan and assignment program depend less upon next year's prospective need for personnel than upon expected needs a long time in the future. Such a problem does not exist in the traditional general service, which is built on the assumption that an agency may fill its needs at any grade from the employment market with only slight delay.

There is an equal necessity in career systems to plan the careers of individuals in terms of both their assignments and their training, partly to satisfy the present and anticipated needs of the organization, partly to respond to the needs, interests, qualities, and desires of the individuals themselves. In well-developed career systems one finds a phenomenon seldom found in the general service—individual career plans, sometimes projected ten or more years in the future, comprehending nature and place of future assignments, periods off for training, systematic rotation and transfer programs, etc. And though none of the career planning and development programs is yet well developed, most are ahead of the customary general service practice of assigning a person to a job, where he or she sits until "something better comes along" or, if he or she is aggressive, finds and pushes him or herself into a better job. In career systems, there is some effort to plan and schedule movements and assignments from job to job, whereas in the general service (with a few conspicuous exceptions) they are much more subject to chance and to the initiative and aggressiveness of the individual employee. Further, the career systems have in general been in the forefront of training and educational programs for their members, which are likewise planned, formalized, and more frequent. It was not until 1958 that the federal general service possessed even the legal possibility of outside training, and opportunities are even more limited in most state and local jurisdictions.

Some Consequences of Career Systems for General Government

Members of a career system must always work with other personnel within the organization who lack comparable career status—be they clerical, manual, custodial, other professional, or political. To the extent that the system approaches the "ideal," to that extent is it exclusive and preferential vis-à-vis the other employees. When personnel are working together on the same things but under the operations of two distinct systems of employment, there is always the possibility—even the likelihood—of abrasion between them, especially if one claims a near-monopoly of the top jobs, dominating influence on agency policies, and preferential rewards. A price of the sense of unity, cohesiveness, and homogeneity within the career system itself is often friction, difficulties of communication, and low morale with and among other personnel of the agency. In fact, this seems to be a nearly universal phenomenon within all organizations having clearly differentiated career systems. Compare, for example, the *standard* problems of relationships between:

career officers in military establishments, enlisted personnel, and civilians;

academic and nonacademic personnel at universities;

career officers and noncareer administrative personnel just about everywhere;

politically appointed officers and career leaders at the top.

It is more pronounced where the personnel under two different systems have comparable *levels* of education and experience but in *different* fields and bring to bear *different* orientations on the same problems and *different* views of organizational purpose.

A second consequence has to do with flexibility in the utilization of personnel to meet rapidly changing needs. Here the situation is paradoxical. A career system which contains a body of trained and experienced persons can readily adapt itself to certain kinds of changes *in the short run* through quick reassignments, transfers, even movements over thousands of miles. It is uninhibited by position classification and enjoys a degree of loyalty and discipline, sometimes legally enforceable, not common in the general service. But if it is called upon to meet sudden needs requiring different kinds of skills or to anticipate and prepare for basic changes in mission, rapid growth, or re-education, it is very inflexible. Its supply of journeymen and leaders within the system at any given time is largely fixed because of its inhibition against lateral entry. Increases of career personnel for the future must have entered the pipeline years before. The promises given to members of a progressive career through most of their working lives inhibit reductions-in-force.[2] Most of the agencies with career systems have therefore instituted devices for handling fluctuating needs with minimal disturbance to the central career—reserve officer systems, the general civil service, temporary employment, contract personnel, consultants, for example.

A third consequence is a relatively high premium on conformity of individual behavior with the norms and mores of the system, and with the purposes of the organization as they are perceived and defined by those already in the system. The forces pointing toward conformity begin well before appointment. The "image" of the service is framed in the home and in college, particularly in professional school. One's choice of a field of study is the beginning of self-recruitment. The actual selection process, conducted normally under the direction of experienced career system members, should weed out those who are unlikely to conform; indeed, in some fields that is its primary purpose, for knowledge and

---

2. Many of the career services do not even have policies and procedures to govern staff reductions. But the selecting-out procedures of some of them are used for the purpose.

ability are taken for granted on the basis of college degree and passage of professional examinations. Following appointment, most new members undergo a systematic training and orientation course, followed by a more or less extended intern and apprentice program. Again, the nonconformists can be weeded out before their probation ends, while those who remain have better learned the norms and expectations which will frame their living and working style in the future. There is the continuing pressure of supervision by older officers in the service and association with colleagues, re-enforced if necessary by the risks and rewards of efficiency ratings and the promotion system, all controlled by senior colleagues in the system.[3]

The "perfect" careerist in the "ideal" career system, then, thinks, acts, responds, and decides like his or her colleagues; he or she is a "type" and is often so described, technically efficient in the field of activity of the career and according to criteria set by the system. He or she is a supporter and if necessary a defender of the system as the career system is his or her supporter. He or she is likely to seek and to find technically correct solutions to problems, even though the problems may themselves involve elements not contemplated in the technique; they are usually political or social or interpersonal. Where the problem is patently nontechnical, the instinct is to withdraw and avoid "sticking your neck out." He or she is also prone to avoid or withdraw from open disagreements, hostility, and aggressiveness in associations with colleagues; internal confrontations threaten both the system and its individual members.[4]

3. For a particularly perceptive analysis of how these processes operate in one career system, see Herbert S. Kaufman, *The Forest Ranger: A Study in Administrative Behavior* (Baltimore, The Johns Hopkins Press, 1960).
4. In an interesting report some years ago by Chris Argyris on Foreign Service officers and other officers in the State Department, the contrasts between the career and the noncareer officers are described in very comparable terms—and are almost as overdrawn as this paragraph about

A final consequence of career systems is *conservatism*, in the sense of a resistance to change that might weaken the system. I hasten to add that the conservatism of which I speak applies principally to threats of change to the system itself, to its status in the governmental world, and to the destinies of its members. Some career systems, like some professions, may be politically liberal and amenable to social change.[5] Some indeed are in the business of inventing and bringing about change—as, for example, those in research and development laboratories or on college faculties. Yet with regard to the *institution* of their employment relationship, even these are conservative if they have stabilized and established themselves as members of career systems. Among the older career systems, there is a generally conservative bias toward the subject-matter with which the members of the system deal. This is a product of the constraints against nonconformism and initiative that might be threatening to the system. It is a product also of the way the system operates to produce its leaders. The average age of the top career leaders in most public agencies today is around fifty years. Most of those in career systems will have spent most of their working lives in a single occupational field, many in the same agency. The holding of a single perspective for so long a time—up to forty years—is almost inevitably a sculptor of viewpoints, values, and methods. Insofar as the leaders can impress upon subordinate system members their own views of the world—

---

the "ideal type." Argyris finds the "living system" of the Foreign Service officers, "dominated by a low interpersonal openness, levelling, trust, confrontation; a high withdrawal, mistrust of aggressive, fighting behavior; and a blindness to the superior's negative impact on his subordinates." See his *Some Causes of Organizational Ineffectiveness Within the Department of State* (Washington, D.C., Department of State, Center for International Systems Research, 1966), p. 25.

5. For example, compare the *political* stance of public health officers with doctors generally, or of public foresters with those in private employ.

and as we have seen, the system itself provides effective tools for this—the older perspectives will dominate.

My treatment of the "ideal type" of career service is admittedly extreme and overdrawn. There are probably no systems for which it would be accurately descriptive. One reason for this lies outside the personnel systems themselves: forces in society have prevented career systems from reaching their ideal. They are not "closed" systems. Moreover, contrary forces have compelled the general civil service to move in the direction of career systems. There is thus a tendency for the two to draw closer together, so that neither clearly fits its classical description.

The General Civil Service

We have already seen (in Chapter 5) the tendency of sectors of the general civil service, as they become self-consciously specialized and scientized, to frame themselves more and more as separate, self-contained, professional services. In addition, the general service outside the specialized careers has displayed a tendency to take on some of the accoutrements of careeism and to relax the rigorous application of "rank-in-the-job" and position classification. This tendency has been most marked at the bottom and entry rungs of the public service ladder and at the top. Thus the various general entrance examinations for young college graduates which have developed over the last five decades were designed to attract and select on the basis of career promise, not on specific qualifications for the first job.[6] New recruits normally go through a training or intern program and are also advanced rapidly on a scheduled basis to the journeyman level (usually GS 11 or GS 12 in the federal government). Up until that point there is little significant difference between the general

6. This premise has recently been challenged in the courts. See Chapter 8.

service and the career systems. Position classifications, even beyond these early stages, has been considerably relaxed in various ways: greater recognition of the incumbent's influence on the job; employment of the two-track system of classification and promotion to make possible advancement of scientists and other specialists in technical, nonadministrative work; broadening and generalizing of classes; and others. The concepts of career planning, progressive assignments, in-service training, and development programs are finding their ways into general service systems. The Senior Executive Service, which would itself constitute a career system at the top levels, has generated a good many modifications in the federal government in the treatment of those in executive levels. It may be noted that most of these changes, actual and proposed, have been in the direction of recognizing rank in the person above rank in the job.

Challenges to Career Systems

All the older career systems—and particularly the commissioned corps—have been under considerable strain for many years, especially since World War II. All have changed in response to pressures from outside and within, though sometimes reluctantly and bitterly; and all are in difficulties. The major challenges fall into four main classes: egalitarianism, the knowledge explosion, management, and politics.

In their basic structures the commissioned services, particularly the military and foreign services, survived intact the drive toward *egalitarianism* which characterized much of the nineteenth century and had such impact upon the general civil service. Their staying power may have reflected in part the strength of example and precedent from other nations, and in part the fact that their principal bases of operations were separate from the rest of American society. The relative exclusivity of the corps was supported by geographic separation. Through the nineteenth century and until World War II, the Army and Navy officer groups were dominantly of upper class or aristocratic origins. The great majority were, surprisingly, drawn from rural and small town settings. The South was heavily overrepresented. The division between officers and enlisted men and the importance of rank in both categories were visible and distinct.[7] In the Foreign Service the great majority—both before and after the Rogers Act of 1924—were drawn from upper- and upper-middle-class families, mostly residents of the East Coast, and most were alumni of a handful of Ivy League colleges.[8]

In all the commissioned services the structure of the status system remains, but all have had to yield in a great many ways to demands for *equal opportunity* and *equal treatment*. During and following World War II, as college level education became more and more available to middle- and lower-middle-class citizens, the recruitment base broadened; opportunities for moving from one (lower status) category to another were opened up, and lateral entry was occasionally permitted—or even mandated under pressure from outside the system. Further, extreme differences in the conditions and privileges of the different personnel categories were attacked and considerably reduced. One common device was the setting up of new career systems, more or less modeled on the elite system and with comparable benefits and promises for advancement. Thus noncommissioned officers became a career in the military services; the Foreign Service Staff became a career in the State Department; nurses and social workers acquired their own career statuses in hospitals; and the nonacademic personnel of universities were encom-

7. On these points, see particularly Morris Janowitz, *The Professional Soldier*, Chapter 5.
8. See for example Warren Ilchman, *Professional Diplomacy in the United States, 1779–1939* (Chicago, University of Chicago Press, 1961).

passed in something like career systems. (It is interesting and suggestive that no one has been able to invent a more adequate designation for "nonacademic" personnel; almost their only common attribute is negative: they are *not* in the academic career system. Of course, the same is true of "noncommissioned officers" in the military services.) A consequence of these developments has been the establishment within organizations of whole series of career systems, in many respects comparable with each other but distinct and in some degree separate. And in all, the central, original system remains—and struggles to remain—*elite*, the first among (not quite) equals. It retains, as far as possible, the key jobs with regard to organization policy; it controls, as far as possible, the operating personnel policies of the other career systems; and it monopolizes, as far as it can, the incumbency of the top positions.

In short, the ideal of egalitarianism reached our older career services about a century later than it did the general civil service. It still has some distance to travel, but the issue has been joined and there have been a good many changes.[9] What seems most surprising is the resiliency of the ancient feudal stratification in our career services; no rational observer from Mars could find any reason in the trifurcated personnel structure of the Defense Department (officers, enlisted personnel, civilians). But neither could he understand how the trifurcated organization of Army, Navy, Air Force, each with its own troops, air forces, ships, missiles, and research and development programs, could exist.

A second major challenge to the career systems, new and old, has arisen from the *explosion of knowledge*, both technological and social, since World War II. They have con-

9. There are surprising likenesses between the recent and current efforts to reform (or "democratize") our military and foreign services and contemporary reforms of the civil services in some European countries, such as France.

fronted essentially the same problem in this regard as have the professions in general (Chapter 5). No system built on the premise of bottom-level entry can equip itself internally with the vast array of knowledge and technique to handle, in an effective and up-to-date manner, the problems in its established arena of activities. Further, the growth of knowledge forces fundamental changes in the concept of what that arena actually is and what the system's public mission is. Problems which point up emerging dilemmas abound in almost every area of public activity: police confronted with racial turmoil; school teachers facing classes of underprivileged children and delinquents; diplomats involved in the development of new and only partially civilized countries; Army officers fighting inconclusive wars; Air Force pilots working on projects which will make their wings meaningless; highway engineers seeing their products result in greater traffic congestion. The growth of knowledge has made it apparent that the objectives and the subject-matter of most of the career systems relate to the underlying problems as effects and symptoms, not as core issues. Careerists must work with others in other fields and systems of employment; they must accommodate their own patterns of thought and their own self-definitions to the requirements of collateral systems; and they must equip themselves with knowledge, skills, and points of view which are not provided through the older and traditional training, recruitment, and experience.

The responses of career systems to these kinds of challenges have varied widely. In general, they have been conservative and defensive, giving an inch at a time; and by and large they have been less successful here than in their accommodations to the push toward egalitarianism. The strategies of accommodation include the following.

1. *redefinition of mission,* but this is effective only when accompanied by revisions in content of training and experience for

newcomers and new types of training for those already on the job (illustrated by the Public Health Service, some branches of the military, some mental hospitals).

2. *providing for employment of needed specialists not provided by the career system itself in other categories of employment—*if need be in parallel career systems. (This maintains the "integrity" of the system and, hopefully, the system's dominance of the organization. It is illustrated in the hiring of civil service scientists in the National Institutes of Health, the reserves in the military departments, lecturers and research scientists at universities, and more or less permanent consultants.)

3. *subdividing themselves into specialized subcareer systems while retaining a common cement of doctrine and focus—*such as "leadership" among military officers or "diplomacy" in the Foreign Service.

4. *contracting out to other organizations, private and public, projects and tasks which the personnel of the service is not equipped to perform.* (This is best illustrated in research and development, but applies in varying degree to a wide variety of other activities.)

5. *absorbing into the "career" different types of specialization and experience by lateral entry.* (In the stronger systems this is a last resort which often must be forced from the outside. Lateral entry is a threat to the essence of the system itself.)

The failure of a career system to accommodate to growing knowledge and changing requirements—to redefine its self-image and take steps to give reality to a new one—may lead to a slow and agonizing decline in its control over, and its influence upon, the arena in which it operates. This has happened to some degree in a good many of the diplomatic services of the world, not excluding our own. The challenges to career systems deriving from the knowledge explosion and the accompanying changes in conception of problems, technological and social, are an intensified case of the broader challenge of modifying institutions to keep up with the accelerating dynamics of our culture.

The third kind of challenge to career systems is implicit in the emergence of *management* in public organizations. This is partly a product simply of growth in size of a great many public agencies. More important, it results from a growing realization of the complexities and the ramifications of consequences of public policies and decisions. Few of the career systems and of the professions, established or emergent, which comprise them, gave much if any attention to management (or administration) either in their preparatory education or in their in-service career and training programs. Yet students of administration have known ever since Henri Fayol that the bulk of activity at the upper levels of any sizable organization is managerial, not technical or professional. At and near the very top, technical knowledge and understanding are perhaps an essential background, but the basic content of the job is managerial in its broadest sense. Recent studies of public executives have re-enforced Fayol's argument; and they have shown that management is today much broader and more difficult than the POSDCORB[10] of the thirties. Our public executives are dealing with problems which go far beyond either supervisory leadership or technical proficiency; they concern the social, economic, and political—as well as technical—consequences óf governmental activity. *Management is also policy.*

It is not coincidental that career systems customarily derogate the word and the practice of administration. In the military, the word is equated with the filling out of morning reports; in the Foreign Service, with the hiring of local personnel; in a university, with the treatment of stenographers. The "substantive" content of a career system is the

---

10. An acronym invented by Luther Gulick representing the elements of a chief executive's work: planning, organizing, staffing, directing, coordinating, reporting, and budgeting. See his "Notes on the Theory of Organization" in Luther Gulick and L. Urwick, *Papers on the Science of Administration* (New York, Institute of Public Administration, 1937), p. 13.

valued element; management (or administration) is regarded as a routine, nondiscretionary instrument. At the University of California in Berkeley a leader of the student movement in the 1960s did not arouse much argument from the faculty when he asserted that the job of the administration was to keep the sidewalks clean.

But the career systems are increasingly challenged—and increasingly vulnerable—in this position. A public health officer can hardly defend his position and status by citing his reputation as an M.D. or by noting that as an intern he delivered a dozen babies when his problems concern the pollution of the air, the remedies for atomic exposure, the problems of the underprivileged in kindergarten, and most particularly the mobilization of a variety of resources, public and private, to meet these problems. Except for their widely different subject-matter content, there is little to distinguish the essential problems of the top-level public health officer from those of the welfare director, the military commander, the career ambassador, the highway commissioner, or the dean or president of a university. All are professionally oriented, all are concerned with problems which go far beyond their subject-matter training, experience, and interest. In the future, fewer will be able to respond to public and political demands with the argument that they are *only* doctors, *only* welfare workers, *only* highway engineers, *only* military officers, *only* diplomats, *only* professors, *only* school superintendents and principals. They will be expected to be something more, and the more successful among them will be those who respond positively to that expectation.

The responses of the career systems to the growing importance and widening dimensions of management have, by and large, been grudging and slow. They have included:

1. separation, specialization, and demeaning of "administration," distinct from "substance";
2. establishing what amounts to a "two-track" channel within the career system, one occupying executive and managerial

posts, the other engaged with substantive work of the system (e.g., Janowitz's distinction between "heroic leaders" and "military managers," or the increasingly recognized distinction between "scientist administrators" and practicing scientists);[11]

3. bringing in "experts" in managerial fields but in subcareer systems or in the general service, while maintaining direction and control by system members over their activities;

4. introducing general social and managerial considerations and criteria into the system itself—in education, selection (including lateral entry), training, assignments, promotions.

The fourth challenge to the career systems, which is here labeled the *political challenge,* is in a sense a summation of the others (egalitarianism, the knowledge explosion, and management). For politics has provided one of the principal vehicles—sometimes the final and decisive one—whereby the others are articulated and effectuated within career systems.

In its narrow sense, politics is and always has been the natural enemy of career systems. Most such systems grew up in opposition to and as a defense against political intrusion. Politics constitutes a standing threat, even when quiescent, against the very elements which are most central to a system's values: security of members' status and tenure; self-government; standards of entry, as well as the policy against lateral entry; standards for advancement. One might hypothesize that those career systems which are best established, most widely recognized, and grounded in the most esoteric fields of knowledge are least endangered by politics. But none is completely protected all the time and under all circumstances.

If we define politics broadly to include those processes whereby interests and influences are mobilized and articulated to change or defend public policies and programs, its importance for career systems in relation to democracy is great. Large and important areas of policy are of course within the

11. Op. cit., especially Chapter 2.

purview of individual agencies that are largely dominated by members of career systems. The development and effectuation of changes in policy thus inevitably depend upon the abilities, perspectives, values, and strategies of political leaders who are not themselves "of the career." There is a wide variety of channels through which advocates of change can operate: legislative investigations and consequent publicity; the media; legislative committees and their staffs; executive task forces and other study groups, usually composed largely or entirely of members, public and private, who are not in the career system directly affected; legislation; executive directives; appropriations; whistle-blowing; and appointments and promotions to leadership posts, not only of political overseers of the career system but also of career members themselves.

Yet major changes in direction may often be successfully resisted and frustrated by a strongly entrenched career system which opposes them, even if, in opposing, it leaps the hurdles of laws and budgets and executive orders. The naming of a policy or a program does not make it live. Indeed, new policies depend heavily, in both development and effectuation, upon the cooperation and support of the career system and particularly of its leaders. Frustrated advocates of change are likely to turn their attention—after a few failures—to an attack upon the recalcitrant career system itself, its leadership, and its established modes of operating. It seems likely that most significant changes in career systems have originated outside the systems themselves or from threats and fears of outside action. They include the broadening of the recruitment base; the insistence upon admitting to the "club" persons with different types of background and orientation; the revision of promotion criteria; and the reduction in distinctions and privileges between the elite members and other employees within the same agency. They include the practice of dipping down into the system by political officers to select for leadership posts those career officers who are sympathetic to the aims of the political leadership and who may also be "unorthodox" system members. The refusal of the Senate to act on the Navy's promotion list until the name of Admiral Rickover was added is an excellent example of the use of a political instrument to attack the fabric of a career system's promotion policy.

Career systems, of course, are not exactly powerless against this kind of attack. Many of them carry a great deal of prestige in the eyes of the public and in political circles. Many have strong friends in both executive and legislative branches, and a few command the support of enormously powerful interest groups.

Most of the time, too, they are supported by the negative force of inertia. It is much easier not to change than to change, and only occasionally can a head of political steam be built up for "reform" of a system. They are most vulnerable in times of emergency for their agency, sometimes following a dramatic failure, and during a period of political transition following a change of party control through election. The first is illustrated by the military systems preceding and during a war; the Foreign Service during diplomatic crisis; welfare, police, and schools after an urban riot. The second has been abundantly illustrated following the election of an Eisenhower or a Kennedy or a Reagan. These turnabouts were times of trouble for many career systems.

The Political Executives

A principal instrument of change for career systems and for the general civil service is through the appointments to executive posts of outsiders who are presumed to be more directly responsive to the wishes of elected executives and legislators. I refer here to those whom the literature now describes as *political executives*, who, for present purposes, may be simply defined as official appointees outside any protected civil service or career system who significantly influence public policy or direct important governmental programs.[12] There is so little governing doctrine or accepted practice about political executives in American governments that it is all but impossible to generalize about them. (Some who are so described are not political; some are not executives; and some are neither.[13]) As here understood, they have in common only 1. that they have a significant influence on the course of government activity and 2. that they have no insurance in their jobs; indeed a good many of them, particularly those at higher levels, are unlikely to survive an election which overturns the party controlling the executive branch. Many of them do not expect or want to stay in their positions very long, and this expectation is shared by others in the government and in their agencies. But here again, there is contradiction: some expect to and do stay in their posts indefinitely, even when they lack any legal protection or tenure.

In the national government, there are about 2000 persons in the Senior Executive Service or higher, most of whom observers would characterize as political executives, but the number would no doubt vary widely depending upon one's definition of "executive." Some of these are appointed by the President; the rest by his appointees. In state and local jurisdictions, it is probable that many of the larger governments in industrialized areas have political executives in roughly

12. The definition is adapted from that of Marver H. Bernstein in *The Job of the Federal Executive* (Washington, D.C., The Brookings Institution, 1958). The more recent work by Hugh Heclo, *A Government of Strangers: Executive Politics in Washington* (Washington, D.C., The Brookings Institution, 1977) appears to avoid a quick definition; instead, much of the book is itself a definition.

13. I do not include in this treatment political appointments to nonexecutive posts (like U.S. Marshals) nor temporary appointments to nonpolitical posts.

parallel capacities and proportions; but some have far fewer who are political because of the pushing of civil service coverage protections upward (as in Los Angeles and the state of California), and some have far more because of the absence of civil service protections. The massive turnovers in our national administrations, not only of executives but also of their secretaries, chauffeurs, and clerks, are astonishing, even appalling to observers from other countries with western traditions and even those in Communist and third world countries—apart from political revolutions.

There is no ready and clear-cut criterion for classifying political executives, but for purposes of discussion, I would suggest four echelons, depending somewhat upon the criteria and procedures involved in their appointments, the nature and extent of their responsibilities, and the direction of their loyalties. My prototypes are drawn from the national government, but to varying extents they probably apply also to the larger state and local jurisdictions.

First among these are *the immediate political associates* of the chief executive, those in his political and perhaps personal family, who are appointed (usually without confirmation by any outside body) to top positions in the White House (or its equivalent) or work there even if unpaid or if paid by some other agency. Some of these are the most powerful officials and also the least politically responsible, except through the chief executive himself. Some are virtually unknown. Recent history—the last forty years—suggests that not many have had much previous experience in running the whole or any part of the national government, or even a large organization of any kind. They are selected because of personal or professional friendship and trust gained through prior association in the private (or in some cases public) sphere and, very often, in the political campaigns through which the chief executive was nominated and elected. The chief executive and his immediate personal lieutenants are likely, at least at the beginnings of their terms, to have little knowledge or acquaintance with the problems, institutions, and people they will be dealing with. And a good many of these lieutenants may be quite innocent of public issues and ideologies; they are far more knowledgeable about the techniques of getting a candidate elected.

The second category of political executives consists of those chosen as heads of the major departments and agencies, as members of commissions, and as ambassadors to important and friendly countries. Most of these appointees must be confirmed by the Senate or other senior branch of the legislative body and must stand publicly and officially for the programs and budgets they espouse for their agencies. In some ways, these appointments are the most important acts a president or governor, mayor or city manager may make. Partly this is because the kinds and qualities and capabilities of these appointees strongly indicate the quality and the nature of public administration which will follow. Partly it results from the reflection it provides on the ideology, the policy inclinations, and the quality of the executive himself. As a saying goes: "By his appointments shall ye know him." Most of the appointees at this level are relatively generalist in their qualifications and experience, relatively well-to-do, and sympathetic with the ideology of the chief executive. At the national level, if they are Republican, most of them will be millionaire businessmen and lawyers, perhaps tempered, as by an Eisenhower appointment, with a plumber. If the president is Democratic, he will probably appoint one or two Republicans, some college professors, as well as businessmen and lawyers. Presidents of either party may appoint a top career man (a Marshall or a Haig) and perhaps several who have had experience in prior administrations of the same party—but usually not in the same position.

There has been a considerably increased tendency to appoint college professors but it is doubtful that this constitutes a trend. Six of President Johnson's cabinet at one time

had been college professors. Second to lawyers, the largest
professional group in cabinet positions has been economists.[14]
Almost half of all Presidential appointments of cabinet secretaries and their deputies between 1952 and 1980 had law
degrees. Almost nine out of ten of those appointees had
earned at least a four-year college degree, and, leaving aside
those with degrees in law, the majority of those with bachelor
degrees had also earned degrees at the doctoral or master's
levels. Most of these appointees supported the President in
his political campaigns, but few were active politicians in
the usual sense. This contrasts with the middle and later
nineteenth century, when nine tenths of all cabinet appointments were lawyers—then nearly synonymous with politicians. There seems to be a general rule, infrequently violated,
not to appoint to one's cabinet persons who have challenged
or might in the future challenge the chief executive in the
political arena.

The third echelon of political executives is the subcabinet level: the assistant secretaries, assistant administrators
of noncabinet agencies, chief administrators of the larger
commissions, general counsels, and a few others. These are
likely to be at least as well educated as their cabinet-level
superiors, and more specialized in their training and experi-

14. See Steven E. Rhoads, "Economists and Policy Analysis," *Public Administration Review,* 38 (1978), p. 113. The record of appointments of
cabinet secretaries and their deputies by the six presidents, Eisenhower
to Carter, that Rhoads compiled was:

	Law Degrees	Economists PhD	Economists MA	Other PhD	Other MA/MS	All Other	Total
Carter	9	3	2	2	0	8	24
Ford	14	3	1	2	3	8	31
Nixon	24	7	0	3	3	17	54
Johnson	14	2	0	2	3	4	25
Kennedy	17	0	0	0	2	6	25
Eisenhower	13	1	1	1	3	15	34
Total	91	16	4	10	14	58	193

ence—specialized in fields considered appropriate to their governmental assignments. But the majority are probably still generalists with widely varying experience in government, business, and professions.[15] Partisan political considerations may be somewhat more important for many in this category than for their superiors, and some are designated because of pressures from the Congress and the administration party. Relatively few are or have been active politicians, but loyalty to the party, to its prevailing ideology as defined by the chief executive, to the President, and in widely varying degree, to the top secretary or administrator of the agency are important considerations. The Mann and Doig study referred to in footnote 15 suggested a high degree of mobility in the experiences of assistant secretaries. A majority had prior experience, sometimes very extensive, in governmental service, especially federal, and nearly half had been career civil servants. The subcabinet group may offer the best promise of a two-platoon system in American administration comparable to that found in some parliamentary countries: groups of experienced executives in each party who might be called upon to participate in the administration of government when their party is in control.

The departments and agencies have not been consistent in the ways in which they use assistant secretaries and assistant administrators. All use some of these positions in essentially staff roles where they have jurisdiction over certain kinds of

---

15. These observations about assistant secretaries are synthesized from three sources: Thomas P. Murphy, Donald E. Nuechterlein, and Ronald J. Stupak, *Inside the Bureaucracy: The View from the Assistant Secretary's Desk* (Boulder, Col. Westview Press, 1978); Dean E. Mann with Jameson Doig, *The Assistant Secretaries: Problems and Processes of Appointment* (Washington, D.C., The Brookings Institution, 1965); and Heclo op. cit. The Mann & Doig study reported that fewer than 30 percent were appointed on the basis of "expertise" while about 65 percent were appointed for their "general experience." I would guess that the emphasis upon expertise has risen somewhat as the number of positions at this level and the specialization of their assignments have grown.

activities that cross over all or most of the line operations: administration, Congressional relations, public affairs, international affairs, program evaluation, general counsels, and inspectors general. In some departments, assistant secretaries have been put directly in the line between the secretary (and the secretary's deputy or undersecretaries) and operating bureaus or services below. Examples are the Assistant Secretary of Interior for Fish, Wildlife, and Parks, and the Assistant Secretary for Health in the Department of Health and Human Services. Yet it is believed by some that the prestige and influence of assistant secretaries have significantly declined, and it seems to be increasingly difficult to find persons capable and willing to accept them, especially by Republican administrations. This apparently results partly from the growth in staff and strength of the White House and some units in the Executive Office of the President, and their increasing involvement in policy making; partly because of the growth and increasing involvement in administrative decisions, both general and detailed, by Congressional subcommittees and their staffs; partly because of the development of a class of deputy secretaries and undersecretaries between the assistant secretaries and their secretaries.[16]

By far the largest number of political executives are in *the fourth echelon*, a category which includes the deputies and some of the assistants to the secretaries and assistant secretaries, influential advisers, the chiefs of administrations, services, and bureaus within the departments and agencies, regional directors in many agencies, and overseas representatives of a number of agencies. Most of these individuals are in the Senior Executive Service The trend in this century until World War II, heartily endorsed by the Brownlow Committee, was in the direction of filling such posts with career, professional personnel. In more recent decades, par-

---

16. This topic is discussed at some length in Murphy et al., op. cit. Introduction.

ticularly in areas of political sensitivity, the direction of this trend has reversed. More and more these positions are filled by noncareer, rather than civil service, executives. This does not imply that professional and technical expertise is lacking or is less than it was before; only that the top professional leaders enjoy less protection than they once did and that most of the positions of specialists have, perhaps unavoidably, assumed a more political coloration.

In sum, and quite unlike their superiors, the bulk of political appointees below the third echelon—i.e., the service and bureau chiefs, the deputy assistant secretaries et al.—are acknowledged and sometimes widely reputed experts in the fields of the agencies to which they are appointed. As Heclo observed:

> The changing nature of the political executive jobs to be filled has generally favored those with specialized technical abilities rather than those with broad political experience. . . . More than ever before, the presidential appointment of people who are ignorant about complex policies for which they are responsible . . . can mean that important decisions are mishandled or devolve to bureaucrats below.[17]

These political executives in the fourth tier occupy a middle ground between the other political executives and the career executives in their agencies. In comparison with the former, they are more likely to:

be drawn from the career or civil service of their agencies or of comparable agencies in other jurisdictions;

be respected professional leaders in specialisms appropriate to their agencies;

have a longer tenure expectancy in their agency and almost complete confidence of continuing work somewhere in their field of specialization;

17. Heclo, op. cit. pp. 67–68.

view their role as one of furthering the interests and programs of
the agencies which employ them;
resist partisan political interventions from above and outside.

Many of these noncareer executives in the fourth echelon
represent their agencies and its career personnel. Some are
eminent figures in their fields, often the principal representatives and defenders of the services which they superintend.
Yet their stance differs from that of the members of the
permanent services below them. They *can* be replaced, or
their situations can be made so uncomfortable as to induce
them to resign or at least to alter their behavior. Political
appointing officers, even when constrained to select bureau
chiefs from within their agencies, can usually find individuals
sympathetic to their program views. Very probably, every
sizable career system harbors some dissidents and nonconformists.

As one proceeds down the four echelons described above—
immediate office of chief executive (White House), cabinet,
subcabinet, and political administrators and advisers at lower
levels—there appears to be a fairly consistent direction
according to a number of different criteria. One is from
political (reelection, and presidential and party interests) to
professional and technical; another is generalist to specialist;
a third is governmental experience, from very low to quite
high; a fourth is expectation of future work in position and
in field, again from low to high; and a fifth is a sense of
loyalty to chief executive and party to that felt toward program and profession. Backgrounds in fields of education and
experience differ radically and progressively. At the top are
general and legal education with a smattering of academic
experience, mainly in economics. In the top two tiers, a
natural scientist, engineer, or physician is a maverick. But as
one goes down the echelons, engineers, physical, biological,
and social scientists along with specialists in various aspects
of administration become more prevalent. The level of edu-

cational attainment is high for all echelons, even though the
fields of study differ widely. Most have at least a bachelor
degree, and there are uncommonly high proportions of
Masters and Ph.D.'s.

Despite recent efforts, especially by President Carter, to
appoint more women and minorities to executive posts, the
group as a whole (if it were indeed a group) would hardly
please an ardent advocate of representative bureaucracy. In
the words of Heclo again, political executives are "dispro-
portionately white, male, urban, affluent, middle-aged, well
educated at prestige schools, and pursuers of high-status
white-collar careers."[18]

It may very well be that in our kind of scattered and
pluralistic society, our mode and differentiation of political
appointments, never consciously planned, is desirable, possibly even inevitable. We have somehow invented a politico-
administrative system resembling a farm on a steep hill,
protected from violent damage in a political storm by a series
of terraces, each interrupting and delaying a downpour and
thus saving the farm. At the topmost terrace is the purely
political (winning the last election or the next one); at the
bottom are the farm and those who work it—the career
personnel. In between are the terraces of oversight, guidance,
and two-way communication, which also protect the farm
from destruction in a cloud-burst.

This series of terraces may be the best bridges we have yet
devised to connect politics and administration. But this
agricultural allegory is here idealized. It probably works
nowhere all of the time and, in some places, none of the time.
Where there is an irreconcilable difference in ideology between top and bottom, the terraces may slow the destruction
of the farm and the flight of its career personnel, but not
prevent them. And when a new administration fails to fill
the intervening political levels or fills them with people

18. Ibid., p. 100.

improperly qualified and motivated, the consequences are likely to include: poor communications both ways; failures of understanding; suspicion and mistrust; uninformed decisions on top and conflicting decisions down below; and misdirection or outright sabotage of programs, subtle or sometimes overt.

This chapter has analyzed and contrasted three types of systems of employment: the career systems, the civil service systems, and the political systems. Most of the larger public agencies contain at least two of them, and the majority contain all three. Each provides somewhat different types of persons, orientations, perspectives, skills, and knowledge. Each has its own distinctive view of responsibility, of representativeness, and of what constitutes the public interest. The interplay among them may be the most interesting and crucial element in America's political democracy—especially near the top where decisive issues are negotiated, debated, and resolved or tabled.

There is little agreement as to what kinds of positions should be covered within which system and what roles and powers their incumbents should exercise. Most of them have developed without a discernible rationale, and there is wide variation in personnel systems among different jurisdictions of government and among different agencies within each. The dangers of any system passing outer limits are clear. Where political appointments invade too far the province of the respective career services, there is a threat to substantive effectiveness, an invitation to inefficiency and even scandal. Where the political appointees are driven out, there is a threat to the general interest in favor of special interests, to "the public" in favor of a self-directed or entrenched bureaucracy. American history provides abundant examples of both types of dangers.

All the systems bring a certain kind of yeast to the dough of public management. The permanent services provide the advancing knowledge and technology, the responses to clients, the more intimate acquaintance with program needs and operations. The higher echelons of the political appointees bring fresh views on social needs (beyond those of specific clienteles), political and party leadership, and a restless desire to question, to change, and to improve. The crucial problems occur at those places where the differing groups come together, must find bases of communication and understanding, must compromise and agree on actions. I refer here to the relations of political and career personnel generally; of career system and other civil service personnel in the same agencies; of the four different strata of political personnel described above; and of all of them with organized unions which are treated in the following chapter.

But the wholesale turnover of political officials whenever there is a transition from one chief executive to another, especially when they are of different political parties, is a source of almost unbelievable extravagance, disorder, and inefficiency. This problem and its accompanying waste are most conspicuously evident at the national level of our government, but they occur in varying degrees in other jurisdictions as well. If anything, the problem is becoming more severe as fewer and fewer presidents survive a full two terms, and many are succeeded by presidents of the opposite party.[19] Each such transition means bringing in a new team, which is in no sense a team but a conglomerate of "strangers" (the term of James Madison), many of whom have no prior government experience—other than working on or contributing to electoral campaigns—and no experience whatever in the job they are called upon to perform. Few of these newcomers will, or expect to, stay in their posts very long— possibly two or three years, by which time they may have learned something about it and be happy to use their govern-

---

19. Only three presidents in this century, none since 1960, have survived in office a full two terms: Woodrow Wilson, Franklin D. Roosevelt, and Dwight D. Eisenhower.

mental credentials to seek some occupation that is more lucrative. But it is a process which costs the government its effectiveness half of every four-year term. The first months are spent getting bearings, establishing credibility, learning the problems, beginning on solutions. The middle months are potentially the useful periods in a term (provided the most effective operatives have not already left). The closing months are devoted to preparing for the next election, the primaries, and the election campaign itself.

The impact of this kind of cycle upon the "bureaucracy"—the civil service and the career systems—can be devastating. To uncertainties about program and job are added mutual suspicions, distrust, sometimes hostility between careerist and political leadership. With the general diminution of government and other institutions in popular esteem it has become inviting if not mandatory that aspirants for high elective office, and even incumbents in them, run their campaigns against the established administration, that is, the "bureaucracy." And when they win, they are "stuck with," and almost totally dependent upon, people whom they have been vociferously attacking, a situation hardly conducive to constructive relationships.

It is almost unimaginable that such a system could operate in any other institution in the world. There have probably been occasions in this country when appointments of new presidents by private corporations or foundations have been followed by wholesale removals and replacements of large numbers of top officials. But I doubt that any new university president has seen fit immediately to fire his predecessor's entire personal staff, including his secretaries, plus most or all the vice presidents, deans, associate deans, department chairmen, and then has also insisted that most of the replacements neither have any prior experience in his university—nor indeed, in any university.

How long can the United States and its state and local units tolerate such a system? Or survive with it?

The Collective Services

The founders of civil service did not bargain on collective bargaining. The polemics about civil service reform included no reference to employee organization; they were in fact antithetical to the idea of collective relationships among employees. There was, and there remains, an intense individualism in the civil service ideology. Each competitor should be measured against others by the yardstick of merit. In consequence, most of our governments until recently operated with little experience, little understanding, and little legal basis for dealing with employees collectively through organizations.

At the time of the Pendleton Act and of many of the state civil service laws which followed it, labor organization possessed generally low repute; it was not a significant element in public personnel management. To be sure, a number of blue-collar workers in federal, state, and local governments had been union members half a century earlier—unions organized according to craft and without regard to whether the employer was public or private. In subsequent years labor organizations blossomed and flourished, particularly in the Post Office. But public management—and the ethos of civil service reform—by and large opposed them. Appointment and advancement in the civil service were to be based upon individual merit, and the criteria were not to be adulterated by pressures from associations of employees.

The prevailing posture of the administrative side of most American governments has been indifference or hostility to labor organizations, and indifference toward organizations seeking to exercise influence may be just as damaging as hostility. Only a minority of private employers have so successfully and so long resisted effective collective bargaining as have most governments. Until the 1960s, almost every national administration opposed effective labor organization within government, even while some of them deemed it desirable, even mandatory, in the private sector. Indeed, the Januslike perspectives of a good many of the liberal political leaders on the labor issue during the first sixty years of this century were remarkable. At the same time that they were championing the rights of organinzed labor in industry and commerce, they were ignoring or denying them in government. Thus could the earlier Roosevelt, Theodore, issue his notorious "gag" rules in 1902 and 1906 forbidding employees or employee associations to "attempt to influence in their own interest any [pay legislation or] other legislation whatever, either before Congress or its committees. . . ." The later Roosevelt, Franklin D., sponsor and signer of the "Magna Carta of American Labor," the Wagner Act of 1935, two years later wrote that collective bargaining "has its distinct and insurmountable limitations when applied to public personnel management. The very nature and purposes of government make it impossible to bind the employer in mutual discussions with employee organizations."[1] No president since

1. Theodore Roosevelt's first gag rule was issued in an Executive Order of January 31, 1902. It was amended in 1906 to apply to executive establishments outside the cabinet departments. Franklin D. Roosevelt's statement was contained in a letter of August 16, 1937, to Luther C. Steward, President of the National Federation of Federal Employees. See Murray B. Nesbitt, *Labor Relations in the Federal Government Service* (Washington, D.C., The Bureau of National Affairs, Inc., 1976), p. 11.

the thirties could publicly espouse a repeal of the rights of labor in the private sector to organize and bargain. Until John F. Kennedy, however, none had taken any serious steps toward comparable assurances for public employees; and, as will be noted later, Kennedy's action in 1962 fell a good deal short of labor's guarantees in industry.

This contradictory stance is paralleled by another curious paradox. The cause of organized labor in government is both defended and attacked on the basis of democratic principles. On the one hand the rights to associate, to organize, to exercise such power (subject to certain ground rules) as can be commanded to improve the workers' lot—these rights are held to be inalienable in a democratic polity. On the other hand public employee organizations, it is alleged, pose a threat to democratic rule; to the extent that they can advance the interests of their members, they deprive political representatives, who are responsible to the whole people, of power over public policy. Further, an effective government union or employee association can hardly be neutral on some public issues, nor can its members. Finally, and in most extreme form, a state representing a sovereign people cannot bargain away that sovereignty to single groups of its citizens acting in their own interest. In a democratic polity, policy and administration must ultimately be unilateral from the top down—or bilateral, if one considers the executive and legislature as separate powers. At any rate, it is not trilateral. So the argument runs.

The rationale seems to be losing its relevance. The pragmatics in American history have a habit of brushing aside legal niceties in the rush of events; they have proven again and again the plasticity of constitutions and laws. We have for two decades been in a tornado of governmental labor activity, comparable to the storm that swept the private sphere in the thirties. In some ways, the most intriguing question is: Why has it come so late? What has held it up? Government—more especially the federal government—has often aspired to be a "model employer," in the vanguard of fair practices in the employment field. And not without effect. It has led most employers in the competitive principle, "equal pay for equal work," a retirement system, a minimum wage, and more recently employment of the physically handicapped, and employment opportunities for women and minorities. But with respect to the recognition of labor organizations and truly effective bargaining, the federal as well as most other American governments was about a generation late.

The Heritage to 1962

In state and local governments, unionization and collective bargaining were little developed until quite recently. In some, the employees never won the battle for security in tenure against political spoils. In others, civil service became so strongly entrenched as to inhibit the development of powerful employee unions. In most, unions were discouraged by the essentially conservative cast of state legislatures, city councils, county boards, and boards of education. Unions did, however, develop in parts of the federal establishment, and had a growing influence on federal employment policies. Starting soon after passage of the Pendleton Act, the postal unions played an important part in the passage of the eight-hour-workday law for federal employees in 1888[2] and later, of the Lloyd-LaFollette Act of 1912, which for 65 years remained the most important—indeed almost the only—law asserting and protecting rights of federal unions. Later joined by a service-wide union—the National Federation of Federal Employees (NFFE)—the unions were influential in the passage of the Retirement Act of 1920 and the Classification Act of 1923.

---

2. The first permanent union in the Post Office, the National Association of Letter Carriers, was formed in 1888.

Subsequently union influence seems not to have grown except in certain pockets of the federal service. Federal unions have contributed support to a number of measures designed to strengthen the merit system and benefit civil servants (such as the Welch Act of 1928, the Postmaster Act of 1938, the revisions of the Retirement Act, and a variety of fringe benefits and pay acts). Federal unions have also dampened a number of efforts to damage the civil service. Their aims were fundamentally the same as those of the civil service; unions had with civil service the common enemy of partisan patronage. Civil service provided a guarantee of tenure and security and an orderly, predictable system for personnel decisions. Government unions therefore worked within the civil service system, contributed their support to its extension, and sought to maximize their influence in the civil service organizations. Few of them were in any sense radical.

In some organizations the unions came to exercise great influence on employment practices. Largest among these was the Post Office (since 1970, the U.S. Postal Service) with its tremendous, widely scattered, and politically influential labor force, the great majority of whom have long been unionized. Second were the industrial establishments of military and a few other agencies where the craft unions of the private sector have been active. Third were a few federal agencies in which management deliberately encouraged unionization and collective bargaining. Notable among these was the Tennessee Valley Authority (TVA).

Yet for the bulk of federal employees outside the Post Office Department, employee organization was weak if not totally unknown. President Kennedy's Task Force, discussed below, reported in 1962 that one third of all federal employees belonged to labor organizations—a proportion almost exactly equal at that time to that of nonagricultural employees in the private sector. About three fifths of the fedearl union members were postal workers, and more than half of the others were blue-collar workers. Obviously the unions had made only minor inroads among the main body of white-collar federal employees outside the Post Office—something in the order of 15 percent.

This apparently low level of unionization in the federal government is illusory. White-collar employees were not widely unionized in the private sector either. Employee organizations have not thrived in the service industries, and much of government is service oriented. On balance, one would guess that among comparable groups of employees (blue collar, clerical, professional, and administrative), unionization of federal employees was no less common than in private organizations. But government unions lacked the collective bargaining guarantees of a Wagner Act; most of them disavowed the use of the ultimate weapon—the strike; few could assure prospective members of effective influence upon the central issues of labor relations: wages and hours.

If union membership in federal employment was equivalent to that in the private sector, the acceptance of collective bargaining was not. Mrs. B. V. H. Schneider attributed this not to any theory of sovereignty or other peculiarity of public employment, but to a simple behaviorial fact: "At no time have a sufficient number of federal civil servants believed that bargaining rights were desirable or necessary and been prepared to press for such rights."[3] The statement is no doubt true, but it does not explain *why*. I would hazard as one reason that the bulk of federal employees were professional or clerical, and these categories had nowhere been aggressive in collective bargaining. A second reason is that the middle and lower grades of the federal service have, on the whole, done pretty well with their wages, hours, and fringe benefits without the necessity of labor organization. For political reasons, and perhaps partly as a spin-off from the aggressiveness of the postal unions, personnel in the lower levels of the

---

3. "Collective Bargaining and the Federal Civil Service," *Industrial Relations,* 3 May 1964, p. 98.

federal service have for many years been in a favorable position relative to other employees. Their pay has been relatively high, their hours reasonably low, their vacations relatively generous, their positions secure. The incentives for unionization and collective bargaining in such circumstances would almost certainly be minimal. The personnel who were relatively disadvantaged in federal (and much state and local) employment were those in middle- and upper-level professional, scientific, and administrative positions, mainly because of the well-known compression of salary rates.

A third reason is found in the linking, by the public and by prospective union members, of labor organization with its more extreme weapons, particularly the strike, coupled with the general fear and disapproval of their use against "vital" public activities.[4]

In any case until the 1950s and 1960s there was a relatively quiescent labor presence in most of government, one which —with sporadic exceptions—made modest demands and little public noise. Effective systems of collective bargaining, systems in which both parties had sufficient power to influence settlements, were few and far between.

The Labor Explosion of the 1960s and 1970s

Against so sleepy a backdrop, the recent development of labor organization and collective bargaining in government was both sudden and unexpected. It was probably fed in part by the rapid growth of state and local employment, in part by the increasing disposition of subprofessional and professional personnel to organize and endeavor to improve their lot. But behind it also has been the fundamental anomaly of governments' supporting and requiring practices in the pri-

---

4. Though Leonard White showed long ago that many services in the private sector were as vital as some in the public—or more so. See his "Strikes in the Public Service," *Public Personnel Review*, January 1949, pp. 3–10.

vate sector, which they discouraged or denied for their own employees. In the words of the American Bar Association in 1955:

> A government which imposes upon private employers certain obligations in dealing with their employees may not in good faith refuse to deal with its own public servants on a reasonably similar basis, modified of course to meet the exigencies of public service.[5]

Changes began, as has so often been true of public reform movements in the past, at the municipal level. Several of the larger cities piece by piece negotiated agreements with unions of various kinds and coverage during the fifties and early sixties: Philadelphia, Cincinnati, Hartford, Detroit, New York, and many others. In 1959, Wisconsin by state law launched its now-famous program authorizing and prescribing methods for collective bargaining in cities (though not then in the state government itself) and providing that a state agency, the Wisconsin Employment Relations Board, supervise its operations. The Wisconsin system was the nearest approach in the nation for public personnel to that provided by the National Labor Relations Act for private employees.

The federal government came along a little later. In fact, Congress had under consideration, in almost every session from 1948 on, one or more bills which would have recognized federal employee organizations. Most of them would have guaranteed union recognition and collective bargaining with relatively severe penalties for administrative officers who infringed upon such rights. Lacking administration support, the bills made no headway.

Senator John F. Kennedy strongly supported these bills and testified in their behalf. But soon after he became President in 1961, he moved to preempt authority over labor-management relations in the executive branch and effectively

5. *Second Report of the Committee on Labor Relations of Governmental Employees*, 1955, p. 125.

undercut the Congressional initiative. His undercut would silence the Congress in this field for more than fifteen years. Kennedy's first move was to establish a task force to study and make recommendations on labor-management relations in the federal service. In his memorandum setting up the task force, the President made it very clear that in his view federal employees had a *right* to organize and to bargain; and by his appointments to the task force, including particularly then Labor Secretary Arthur J. Goldberg—long-time counsel to the CIO and the Steelworkers Union—its chairman. Kennedy made it clear that he expected an approach fundamentally similar to that in private industry. The task force report, issued on November 30, 1961,[6] contained an expectably enthusiastic endorsement of the right of federal employees to organize and through their organizations to negotiate with their managers, along with a variety of recommendations as to how this right should be exercised. Most of its recommendations were embodied six weeks later in President Kennedy's Executive Orders 10987 and 10988 of January 17, 1962. The Kennedy orders provided a highly decentralized system for union recognition and negotiation in the departments and agencies under very general guidance from the Civil Service Commission and the Department of Labor. In most respects these orders were pale reflections of what was even then standard and required practice in private industry: the scope of negotiation—i.e., what was negotiable; union security; powers of unions; management rights; absence of a supervisory and appellate agency in any sense comparable to the National Labor Relations Board (NLRB). In fact, the Kennedy orders contained no provisions that were not already practiced by one or more different agencies in the federal establishment.

Nonetheless, these orders were probably the most signifi-

---

6. President's Task Force on Employee-Management Relations in the Federal Service, *Report.*

cant event in the history of labor relations of American governments. They established the general legitimacy of the unionization of public employees and of collective bargaining between such employees and public management even though for years the words "collective bargaining" and even "unions" were carefully avoided in federal pronouncements; the preferred terms were "employee-management cooperation" and "employee organizations." They sparked a tremendous growth in the unionization of federal employees which continued through the 1970s; an expansion of the political power of government unions and their leaders; an increase in employee influence upon employment policies and actions in individual agencies; and a growing threat to the principles and practices of both civil service and other types of merit personnel administration.

Every President after Kennedy, at least to the close of the 1970s, took or tried to take some action with regard to collective bargaining in the federal government, and most of the changes were in the direction of increasing the voice and influence of organized labor. Lyndon Johnson in 1967 designated a President's Review Committee on Federal Employee-Management Relations, headed by then Secretary of Labor W. Willard Wirtz. That Committee's proposals, perhaps the most far-reaching of any before 1978, were vigorously resisted by Secretary of Defense Clark Clifford, principally because the report's proposed Federal Labor Relations Panel would be authorized to make final decisions, binding on his own department. The report was published in early 1969 as a draft in the annual report of the Labor Department, but, for want of consensus, it never reached the President's desk.

Soon after his inauguration, Richard Nixon appointed a Study Committee to make recommendations in this area. Many of the recommendations of this group's report, which was transmitted in August 1969, were similar to those of the Wirtz group though distinctly more conservative and more negative toward labor. They were largely incorporated in

Nixon's Executive Order 11491, October 29, 1969, which superseded Kennedy's order 10988. The Nixon action provided for greater centralization over collective bargaining, which virtually everyone agreed was needed, by establishing a general oversight and policy-making body, the Federal Labor Relations Council (FLRC), consisting of top federal officials.[7] Among many other changes, the Nixon order provided only one form of recognition—exclusive—for unions, and this could be gained only by a majority vote in a secret election. The FLRC was empowered to issue binding arbitration decisions. The Kennedy order had provided only for mediation to settle unresolved disputes. Nixon's order also established a Federal Service Impasse Panel within the FLRC and empowered it to issue binding arbitration rulings, subject to appeal to the FLRC. The 1969 order also gave the Assistant Secretary of Labor for Labor Management Relations authority to resolve disagreements over representation rights, the composition of bargaining units, supervision of representation elections, rulings on alleged unfair labor practices, and certain other matters.

Although Executive Order 11491 provided significant advances for organized labor, it was soon under criticism from the unions as well as other groups, including the American Bar Association. Labor was dissatisfied with the absence of opportunity for judicial review (because the executive order was not a statute) and limitations on the areas of negotiation, severe strike restrictions, prohibition of the union shop, and perhaps most of all the relationship of the FLRC to the President. Labor leaders believed that the FLRC could not administer a fair program because it was created and ap-

---

7. After 1971, the FLRC was chaired by the chairman of the Civil Service Commission and included the Secretary of Labor and the Director of the Office of Management and Budget. Such a board might compare, in the private sector, with a National Labor Relations Board consisting of the chairmen of the boards of the Chamber of Commerce, the National Association of Manufacturers, and the Chase Manhattan National Bank.

pointed by, and reported and was answerable to, the President. A few years later, the FLRC conducted an intensive review of the operations of the labor relations program, which resulted in Executive Order 11838, issued on February 6, 1975, by President Ford. This order clarified and strengthened the system as set up by Nixon's earlier order and broadened the scope of issues permitted for bargaining. It did not, however, alter the fundamental organizational problem posed by the FLRC as a management-oriented arbiter and decider.

This problem was one of the central issues attacked by President Carter's civil service reform task forces, described earlier in Chapter 4. His Reorganization Plan No. 2 of 1978 and the Civil Service Reform Act which followed it did not greatly change the rights, the procedures, and the practices which had developed in labor-management relations over the preceding fifteen years. But the Reorganization Plan and the Act did fundamentally change the central structure for overseeing those matters. They replaced the FLRC with an independent, full-time, three-member Federal Labor Relations Authority (FLRA), to be appointed by the President with confirmation by the Senate. They transferred to this new organization the responsibilities of the FLRC and also of the Assistant Secretary of Labor for Labor Management Relations. They created a General Counsel to the FLRA who would investigate and, when appropriate, prosecute alleged unfair labor practices before the FLRA. And they authorized judicial review of FLRA decisions in most cases.

Labor leaders did not get all they wanted, which included repeal of the Hatch Act and a union shop. But they did pretty well. Further, the ambiguous mission of the old Civil Service Commission was clarified. As the Office of Personnel Management (OPM), it was made quite definitely the director and coordinator of administrative policies toward organized labor; it now became unequivocally the arm of management in matters of labor relations.

This sporadic but consistent growth in the influence of unions was accompanied by a steady increase in federal union membership, which nearly doubled between 1960 and 1980. By the latter year, almost three fifths of all federal civilian employees were members of unions or comparable employee associations, and nearly nine tenths of those members were covered under collective bargaining agreements. These figures do not include about 600,000 employees of the U.S. Postal Service, almost all of whom are unionized. When the Postal Service was created in 1970 to replace the Post Office Department, the postal employees were separated from regular federal coverage and placed under the jurisdiction of the National Labor Relations Act.

Very probably, an important spinoff of the federal decisons to recognize and encourage unions and collective bargaining was the impetus they gave to the movements already underway in state and local governments, particularly local. Since World War II, these have grown at a faster rate than any other sector of the country, although their growth rate is now leveling off. With the federal government, state and local governments have also been the fastest growing group in the proportions of employees who hold membership in unions and in employee associations, most of which behave like unions. The proportion of unionized state and local employees was recently estimated at 35.5 percent.[8] The rapid growth in public sector unionism has accompanied stability or relative decline in union membership in the private sector. A recent study revealed that between 1968 and 1976, bargaining organizations in manufacturing industries lost 755,000 members while those in other parts of the private sector gained 781,000 members and public sector member-

8. Washington, D.C., U.S. Department of Labor, Bureau of Labor Statistics, 1980. Figures are for 1980 as quoted by Myron Lieberman, *Public Sector: A Policy Bargaining Reappraisal* (Lexington, Mass., Lexington Books, 1980), p. 4.

ship grew by two million.[9] For a good many years, the fastest growing union in the country has been the American Federation of State, County, and Municipal Employees (AFSCME). Closely following has been the American Federation of Government Employees (AFGE, mainly federal). Both are affiliated with the AFL-CIO, as is the American Federation of Teachers. The National Education Association, which like a number of other professional associations has become a de facto labor union, now has nearly two million members. Among these four organizations alone are nearly four million members, virtually all of whom are government employees.

By the time of this writing, most of the states, particularly in industrial areas, have gone well beyond the federal government in encouraging and extending the limits of collective bargaining, especially for their local governments. A few, mainly in the south, prohibit or severely limit it. Yet in recent years, the fastest growing, the most articulate, and frequently the most militant of labor organizations have been in the public sector. It is at least interesting, whatever one wishes to make of it, that while the size, importance, and political influence of the labor movement in this country have apparently declined in the last couple of decades, public service unions have risen in all these dimensions. Union membership in the private sector, following the National Labor Relations Act in 1935, grew from 6.7 percent of the work force to a peak of 25.5 percent in 1953. Since then, while its numbers have remained steady, its proportion of the work force has steadily declined to 16.2 percent in 1978. Meanwhile, since the late 1950s, membership in public sector unions and associations has been rising sharply, reaching a proportion of the total labor force in 1978 of 5.8 percent,

9. John F. Burton, Jr., "The Extent of Collective Bargaining in the Public Sector," *Public Sector Bargaining*, eds. Benjamin Aaron, Joseph R. Grodin, and James L. Stern (Washington, D.C., The Bureau of National Affairs, 1979), p. 36.

about one third of all employees in the public sector.[10] With the growth in membership has come a growth in the militancy of public employee unions. In defiance of prohibiting laws, they have indulged in strikes, sit-ins, and walk-outs. And for the most part, they were not penalized for such illegal activities until President Reagan cracked down on the air traffic controllers in the summer of 1981.

How Is Public Service Different?

In the social sphere it often takes theory and principle a long time to catch up with practice and "common sense." Scholars and most of the rest of us have long accepted the proposition that public employment is different from private, that the approved norms of the industrial sphere cannot apply to civil servants. The argument was usually buttressed by a number of reasons, among which sovereignty was central. The growing public-private mix of social enterprise through a vast array of mechanisms makes it difficult to draw lines, as the aspirations of workers make it difficult to differentiate rights and expectations of workers in public or private employ. The current rapidity and disparity of change make observation unreliable, prediction risky. The paragraphs that follow undertake no theoretic analysis of sovereignty and the rights of labor. Rather, they are meant to elucidate the practical problems in the governmental realm of labor organization and collective bargaining that are visible today and that demand resolution in the future. One thing is clear: civil service systems and collective bargaining are different. They arise from different ideologies, espouse different aims and values, pursue different procedures. How are they to be reconciled?

A first category of problems centers on the question: *What is negotiable?* The National Labor Relations Act prescribes

10. Ibid., p. 2.

for the private sector bargaining in good faith over "wages, hours, and other terms and conditions of employment"—a blanket stipulation which has been interpreted to cover a very large portion of the labor front. In most American governments at every level, hours, most wages, and some other conditions are determined by a legislative body, not by management. There is legal doubt as to what part of these prerogatives a legislature *can* delegate away (though practice differs among different jurisdictions and among different kinds of employees in the same jurisdiction). In the national government, salary scales for the bulk of employees are established by law or by the President, subject to possible disapproval by the Congress.[11] The same is true of most large jurisdictions. This means that unless the employee organizations bargain directly with the legislatures, their negotiations with management on salary levels can be advisory at the most, for the power to make binding decisions lies elsewhere. Management cannot make commitments in this field, which constitutes the central issue of most labor activity in the private sector. Unions could, theoretically and indirectly, affect salaries on a selective basis through negotiations on position classification. But if there is any sacrosanct element in public personnel administration, it is the integrity of the classification plan, objective and free from pressure. Can classification be made negotiable without shaking the roots of civil service itself?

As a matter of fact, other conditions of employment are often legislated, sometimes in such precise detail as to leave little or no discretion to administrators: criteria for appointments and promotions, hours of work, vacations and other leave, retirement, reductions in force, fringe benefits. It is significant too that most of the causes that employees pursue

11. Exceptions are the blue-collar workers known as wage-board employees, whose wages can be, and in fact are, negotiated in a limited sense; i.e., against the criterion of the prevailing rate.

cost money. Almost everywhere in American governmental life the appropriating power resides in legislative bodies— city councils, school boards, county boards of supervisors, state legislatures, Congress.[12]

In addition to the legislative problems, there are constraints on the administrative side which limit the area of employee negotiation. Some of these, not too unlike those that weighed on the rugged individualists in the private sector five decades ago, relate to the powers and responsibilities of management, its accountability to the people, its exercise of sovereignty. Others stem from the ideology and procedures of civil service. To the extent these are detailed in statute, there is not much that labor can do beyond accepting them or going to the legislature to seek changes in the law. As one city manager put it: "Perhaps most important [of the differences between public and private employment] is that public administrators do not have the same freedom of action which their counterparts in the private sector enjoy. Their authority is conferred on them by public law and by the definition of that law is limited and cannot be delegated or contracted away."[13]

The original Kennedy orders had specified a rather broad range of management rights, which were not negotiable in collective bargaining. These were repeated in the Nixon order of 1969 and later in the Carter Civil Service Reform Act of 1978 with some changes in wording but fundamentally the same substance. According to the Carter legislation, management officials are authorized "to determine the mission, budget, organization, number of employees, and in-

---

12. There are exceptions, especially in the semi-autonomous, self-supporting enterprises such as the Port Authority of New York and New Jersey. The Tennessee Valley Authority is very nearly in this category, and this may have been a necessary condition for the success of its collective bargaining system.

13. Elder Gunter, City Manager of Pasadena, California, in a letter in *Public Personnel Review*, January 1966, p. 57.

ternal security practices of the agency . . . to hire, assign, direct, layoff, and retain employees . . . or to suspend, remove, reduce in grade or pay, or take other disciplinary action . . . to assign work . . . [and] to make selections for appointments" from proper promotion lists or from other appropriate sources.[14] But a section was added to the law which authorized agencies at their discretion to negotiate "on the numbers, types, and grades of employees or positions assigned to any organizational subdivision, work project, or tour of duty or on the technology, methods and means of performing work. . . ."[15]

It should be observed, however, that substantial rights are often reserved to management in private industry, and that individual federal agencies can permit, and have permitted, some or many of these subjects to be covered under collective bargaining agreements. Experience has shown that, even within these limitations, there is an impressive array of subjects that are negotiable.

Clearly, the push of public employee organizations as they grow stronger will be toward exercising greater influence over personnel activities heretofore considered nonnegotiable and retained within the unilateral prerogatives of civil service commissions and other public personnel agencies. Indeed, this movement is already well under way in some places and in certain areas of personnel activity. These areas include appointments, position classification, establishment of minimum examination requirements and class specifications, and promotions. But if these issues, together with others in the legislative domain, remain "off limits" to labor representatives, what is in their domain will not likely satisfy them and their union members very long. Grievance procedures and working conditions not covered by law and the traditional merit system constitute a foot in the door; and the

14. Public Law 95–454, October 13, 1978. Section 7106.
15. Ibid.

door to effective collective bargaining in most public agencies is gradually opening.

In comparing labor activity in the public service with that in private, a second category of problems concerns the *tools* or *weapons* which employee organizations may use. Here, too, there are vital historic and ideological differences, but many of these are now under union attack. Labor organization and collective bargaining were themselves frowned upon in government for most of our history, and they are still forbidden in some jurisdictions. The strike, the anchor power of most unions outside of government, is still forbidden in the national government and a large number of states. So is picketing. Compulsory arbitration of unresolved disputes is not legal in some places. The closed or union shop is not permitted in most jurisdictions; it is probably one of the most difficult of labor's potential tools to square with the principle of equal treatment, long a central tenet of America's merit systems.

In the federal government, employee organizations have won the right to negotiate, to reach written agreements with management, to represent employees in grievance cases, and to have union dues checked off from payrolls. But they lack some of the legal weapons to back up their demands that are available to kindred organizations in private employ. In some local jurisdictions and among some kinds of employees the ultimate weapon, the strike, has been utilized, whether or not legally, without severe penalty. In fact, strikes among local employees have sharply increased. Public sector strikes grew from 15 in 1958 to 481 in 1978; the great majority of them were in school districts and cities.[16] The federal ban on strikes has occasionally been defied; but on the whole it does not appear to be under serious challenge, even by the more aggressive labor leaders. In fact, many seem to regard it as a necessary safety valve in the event of particularly damaging

16. Lieberman, op. cit. p. 35.

strikes in the private sector, which the federal government can terminate through the process of nationalizing a whole industry.

But labor in the public sphere has political weapons not generally available in the private sector. It can and does carry its problems to legislatures and legislative committees. In the federal government and in the large industrial states it can usually expect sympathetic consideration of its views, and through affiliation with larger sectors of the labor movement it can pack a considerable political punch. A major reason that strikes on the local scene have increased so sharply is that local legislative bodies in most jurisdictions have been predominantly conservative. At the national level and in the industrialized states, legislatures are at least as amenable to labor organizations as are the executive branches, and usually more so.

In short, the powers and weapons of labor unions in the public sector are different from those in the private. They are primarily political rather than economic. At the local level the absence of legislative responsiveness has in many places forced employee organizations to utilize the weapons of unions in the private sector. But even there, the major weapon of the strike is essentially a political one. One need not judge whether labor organizations have been more or less effective in the public service than elsewhere, or whether employees have been better treated in government than outside. But clearly their instruments for betterment are different, and it seems reasonable to expect that they will continue to be different.

In comparing collective bargaining in the public and private sectors, the third question is, *Who negotiates for whom?* On the employee side, the situation in government is not unlike that in the private sector forty years ago. There are many different types of organizations operating from different principles with different aspirations, and often they are at war among themselves. They include unions affiliated with the labor movement; unaffiliated unions; craft unions, usually comparable to and affiliated with the same crafts in the private sector; industrial-type unions (like the American Federation of Government Employees and the American Federation of State, County, and Municipal Employees); general employee associations (which are commonly likened by unionists to company unions in the private sector); and professional associations. In general, governments seem to be moving toward the principle of exclusive recognition, long established in the private sector. But uncertainties remain about the definition of the bargaining unit, the handling of situations in which no organization commands a majority, the inclusion of supervisory officials within bargaining organizations, and other issues. With a few exceptions the employee associations—strongest in some of the states—have supported and worked through normal civil service machinery. The industrial-type affiliated unions have been most aggressive and have posed the gravest threat to accustomed public employment practices. Recently, professional associations and unions of professionals in a number of fields have contested bitterly for the right to represent the interests of their professional groups. The unionization of professionals is a relatively recent phenomenon in both the public and the private sectors, and the problems seem to be roughly similar in both.

The question of who will represent labor thus seems not greatly different in the public and the private sectors, except that the former has run several decades behind the latter in crystallizing the issues. One would guess that, in most fields below the professional and supervisory level, affiliated unions will gradually assume primacy as they have for the most part in private industry. Among the professional and subprofessional employees, whatever the outcome of the current struggles between unions and associations, clearly the former are driving the latter toward more aggressive demands and tactics, including strikes.

A difference, even more difficult and crucial, concerns the question of who will represent the employer—i.e., the government—in labor-management negotiations. As we have seen above, the problem here arises first from the separation of powers between executive and legislature. It is complicated, secondly, by the varying degrees of identity and autonomy of individual public agencies, with respect to both the executive and the legislature. Thirdly, the role, power, and degree of autonomy of the civil service organization are a source of ambiguity. Our experience to date at all levels suggests that labor organizations, as they acquire self-identity and recognition, are not greatly influenced by the niceties of political and constitutional theory. They approach the sources of real authority through whatever devices are most promising of results. If present trends toward larger and more influential public sector unions continue, particularly at lower levels of government, we may expect increasing— and increasingly direct—demands upon local legislative bodies. Insofar as these demands are frustrated, the unions will turn to state legislatures to provide guarantees of negotiating rights, minimum standards, and mediating and appellate machinery. Within limits, legislative bodies may delegate, and in many cases have delegated, negotiating powers to administrative officers and special agencies. But the possibilities of appeal back to the legislature can hardly be foreclosed for any organization with potential political power.

The Dilemmas of Civil Service

The rapid growth of labor organizations, like that of the professions, is clouding the already hazy role of civil service agencies. Historically these agencies were the protectors of the public service against the machinations of politics; later, the defenders of efficiency as well as security in the management of public personnel. Public employees turned to the

civil service agencies in both roles as their principal representatives and as proponents of employee interests. The trend
toward legal recognition of employee organizations and of
rights to collective bargaining confronts the civil service
agencies with grave problems. Are those agencies properly
instruments of management with whom labor organizations
should negotiate (short of legislative appeal)? Are they properly representatives of employees in seeking benefits, participation, and adjustment of grievances? Or are they properly
mediators, bringing to bear an objective and disinterested
view and with power to impose, or exert major influence
upon, final judgment? Or are they defenders of traditional
merit system principles against all who challenge those
principles?

The inconsistencies and the conflicts among these roles of
civil service agencies have piecemeal forced differentiation
and separation of roles and functions, a process which is
likely to be extended. This is the logic and the basic merit of
the Carter reforms of the civil service in 1978. The principles
of the merit system and appeals against violations of the system would be decided and defended by an independent
agency, the Merit Systems Protection Board. The fairness of
labor-management relations would be judged by an independent Federal Labor Relations Authority. Both of these
would be collegial, quasi-judicial groups. The development
and enforcement of plans, rules, and standards governing
federal personnel matters would be lodged in an office with a
single head, the Director of the Office of Personnel Management, who would be the agent of the President. He would
also be the principal representative of management in dealing with federal employees and unions.

It seems very likely that, as public employees organize
and become more militant, they are almost bound to cast
civil service organizations in the role of staff arms to management, whatever independence and impartiality may be
claimed. Few at any level of government are likely to be

perceived as NLRB equivalents. Labor organizations may prove a more potent force in driving public personnel administration into the arms of management than the "management movement," epitomized by the Brownlow Committee, ever was. This view was affirmed years ago by a principal public employee union leader: "The role of the civil service commission is not regarded by the workers as that of a third, impartial party; to most of them, the commission is felt to represent the employer."[17]

The organizational question discussed above is but a reflection of a more profound dilemma: the relations between the traditional principles and practices of the merit system and those of collective bargaining. Can the two be made compatible? If public employees are to bargain equally on the conditions of their employment, does this by definition authorize bargaining on the very principles of merit? Obviously, the students and authors who gave rise to the various federal executive orders and the Civil Service Reform Act thought that the two were not in conflict—though they quite consistently opposed provisions for union security (e.g., the closed or union shop) as being threats to merit. It may be noted too that, unlike many state and local jurisdictions, collective bargaining in the federal government does not extend to pay levels, fringe benefits, and a good many other matters considered to be management rights. John W. Macy, Jr., Chairman of the U.S. Civil Service Commission under both Presidents Kennedy and Johnson, wrote that the 1961 Task Force which started it all "faced up to the basic issue of the relationship of the merit system to collective bargaining. It determined that there could be an acceptable compatibility and that the negotiation of agreements with unions gaining exclusive recognition could be developed without violating

17. Jerry Wurf, International President, American Federation of State, County, and Municipal Employees, AFL–CIO, in a letter to *Public Personnel Review*, January 1966, p. 52.

basic merit principles."[18] Others have been less sanguine, one going so far as to say that: "To destroy merit systems . . . is a perfectly logical objective of unions. . . ."[19] In fact, there is a wide divergence of opinion on this question among the many people who have expressed themselves on it. Most would probably agree that if unions took over all the activities to which some of them aspire, which will probably never happen, collective bargaining would replace civil service as we have known it; we would have a quite different definition of merit.

Some of the issues on which there have been or may be collisions between collective bargaining and traditional merit principles are illustrated in Table 2.

In essence, these differences may be reduced to two related issues: first, the extent to which the conditions of employment will be determined on the basis of a bilateral philosophy, which accords the employees a voice equal to that of the employing government; second, the extent to which the terms of employment will be based upon collective as distinguished from individual considerations. The first of these involves basic concessions in the historic concept of sovereignty, the concept that a public job is a privilege and not a right, to the extent that a private job is a right. The second calls for modifications in the ideal of individualism in the merit system as it developed in this country: that each person would be considered on his or her distinctive merits in comparison and competition with all others. The wishes of the individual in relations with his or her employing institution—the government—give way to those of the group acting in concert, a more equal confrontation.

How far and how fast public employment will move in the direction of collective bargaining is problematical. But the

18. John W. Macy, Jr., *Public Service: The Human Side of Government* (New York, Harper & Row, 1971), p. 124.
19. Nelson Watkins in a letter published in *Public Personnel Review*, January 1966, p. 58.

Table 3.

Subject	Collective Bargaining	Merit Principles
management rights	minimal or none; bilateralism	maximal or total; unilateralism
employee participation and rights	union shop or maintenance of membership exclusive recognition	equal treatment to each employee open shop (if any recognition)
recruitment and selection	union membership and/or occupational license entrance at bottom only	open competitive examination entrance at any level
promotion	on basis of seniority	competitive on basis of merit (often including seniority)
classification of positions	negotiable as to classification plan; subject to grievance procedure as to allocation	intrinsic as to level of responsibilities and duties on basis of objective analysis
pay	negotiable and subject to bargaining power of union	on basis of analytically balanced pay plan and, for some fields, subject to prevailing rates
hours, leaves, conditions of work	negotiable	on basis of public interest as determined by legislature and management
grievances	appealed with union representation to impartial arbitrators	appealed through management with recourse to civil service agency

directions are unmistakable. Somewhat surprisingly, among the most aggressive are organizations of professionals or emergent professionals, especially those principally employed by and therefore principally dependent upon public employers: school teachers, social workers, nurses and other hospital specialists, policemen, and firemen. It is worth noting that the concessions now being demanded by the labor movement against unilateralism and individualism are essentially parallel to those demanded by the organized professions and their career services (as described in the preceding chapters). Both constitute challenges to the traditional civil service as we have come to know it. So far, and in most places, the professions have made the greater inroads. But the development of each presents the fundamental confrontation of political and administrative generalism and of personnel specialism by collectivized, organized, occupational groupings.

What does all of this mean for democracy and the public service? A principal argument for collective bargaining, in fact, emphasizes democracy. Bargaining provides the opportunity for participation by those most concerned in determining the conditions and the rewards of their work, for maintaining human dignity in the work situation, for actualizing the self against the stultifying effects of authoritarian rule. In the words of former Secretary of Labor Willard Wirtz: "Collective bargaining is industrial democracy."[20]

Few would challenge the Wirtz definition or argue that, in principle, public employees should be deprived of industrial democracy any more than private employees. Yes . . . but! The defenders of governmental hegemony and of civil service urge that collective bargaining, unless circumscribed by narrow boundaries, threatens political democracy, the ultimate power of the citizen through his political representatives to control the destinies of government and the conditions whereby it employs its personnel.

Clearly there are dangers, but the dangers are on both sides. Those in the private sector are as great as, if not greater

20. W. Willard Wirtz, *Labor and the Public Interest* (New York, Harper & Row, 1964), p. 57.

than, those in the public. A review of the record so far compiled suggests that political democracy has not been seriously threatened by public unionism and collective bargaining except in a few scattered instances. In a great many governmental jurisdictions the wages and conditions of work are substandard; in some they are disgraceful. These can hardly enhance the quality of recruitment and of service, any more than they can improve the worth and dedication of public servants. If unionization and genuine collective bargaining can improve such conditions, it is certainly in the public interest—as well as the interest of the employees—that they be encouraged.

But this calls for an enlightened policy on the part of public employee organizations. Neither the public nor the members of such organizations will be served by policies discouraging initiative, education, training, and dedication to service. The appointment and the reward systems must recognize achievement and promise, not alone union membership and seniority. The most cogent argument against some public unions today concerns not political democracy and popular sovereignty, but their pressure toward conformism and mediocrity.

Finally, it is frequently observed that public employee organizations are increasingly pressing for changes in public policy in, or related to, their particular fields of endeavor. Thus they are infringing upon the prerogatives of elective and appointive officials who are responsible to the public for policy decisions. Their influence on policy at this time is very much less than that of professional groups both inside and outside governmental employ. Nonetheless their influence is considerable, and it is growing. Most employee demands—those regarding wages, hours, working conditions— call for increased expenditures, which in turn necessitate rising budgets and taxes, central issues in American politics. Such demands are often augmented by demands for improved programs and operations: reductions in welfare case loads, reductions in hospital patients per nurse, reduction in pupils per teacher in the classroom. Most of these demands accord with—or fall short of—approved standards set by accredited professional organizations in the various fields. This suggests that the policy aspirations of most employee organizations to this date are neither exorbitant nor unreasonable. Many indeed are minimal in relation to needs and clientele requirements.

At this stage in history, employee organization and collective bargaining offer some promise of greater personal democracy in terms of individual dignity and participation. Their threat to political democracy is scattered, but on the whole seems slight. Their denial would appear contradictory to effective democracy, however defined.

8

Merit, Morality, and Democracy

Over the century separating the second inauguration of Andrew Jackson from the first of Franklin D. Roosevelt, the people of the United States built an ideology which related the public service to their indigenous concepts of democracy in a unique but basically coherent fashion. The ideology came to be known as "merit principles" and the methods devised to give them effect as "merit system." *Merit* became the administrative expression and a foundation of democratic government. As President Theodore Roosevelt said in his first message to Congress in 1901: "The merit system of making appointments is in its essence as democratic and American as the common school system itself." The goals, the norms, and the criteria of merit systems were unambiguous and widely agreed upon. This is attested by the repetitiveness of countless studies at all levels of government which aimed to strengthen democracy through improved personnel practices. Until World War II few such studies failed to recommend extension of civil service coverage, improved competitive examinations, precise job classifications, and "equal pay for equal work." A neutral, efficient civil service was viewed as not merely desirable; it was essential to democracy itself.

Developments since World War II have befogged the meaning of merit principles and confused the content of merit systems. The reasons for this growing ambiguity are partly semantic. No doubt many Americans equate the merit system of employment with trappings and practices inherited from the past and held to be of questionable value and declining relevance today: independent civil service commissions, paper and pencil tests, individual job "ownership," unchallengeable job security, paperwork, red tape. The real sense of "merit principles," however, is a good deal more profound than these stereotyped views, and the doubts about its current applicability go well beyond questions of semantics. They derive from changes in the society, its ethos, its educational system, its vocational strucure—changes so extensive that one wonders whether the old "merit principles" will ever again be operational.

The merit ideology was the progeny of many different parents. Their combination of genes produced an unusual child which, as suggested above, grew into a reasonably solid, consistent, and even handsome adult. Chief among the parents was the Protestant Ethic: respect for, even worship of, work not merely as a practical necessity but as a high moral imperative. As it applies to employment, the word *merit* bears two connotations, both dominantly ethical. One is the sense of deserving and rewarding on the basis of past performance or demonstration (e.g., in competitive examination). Work is fundamentally good, desirable, meritorious; the reward for the deserving is the job or the promotion. The second connotation of merit concerns the grounds or criteria of consideration and judgment. A judge considers an argument on its merits; a scientist considers a proposition on its merits; an employing officer considers a prospective employee on his or her merits. In both usages, merits have to do with considerations of intrinsic, relevant value or truth. Negatively, the considerations scrupulously discard any irrelevancies—whether they be legal technicalities, useless scientific data, or factors unrelated to one's worthiness to perform a job of work. In its early days, merit system reform paid more attention to the negative aspect, the elimination of the irrelevancies, than to the positive. The primary extrinsic (irrelevant) ingredient at the time of the Pendleton Act was politics and patronage, the basic reason for the original civil service reform. But we have experienced many other types of considerations both before and since that time, leading to deviations from merit in personnel administration: military service, geographic representation, sex, race, age, physical handicap, citizenship, national origin, criminal record, level of formal education, other credentials, family relationship (nepotism or its opposite—prevention of government employment of more than one in family), personal friendship (amicism), personality, appearance, need. As job specialism developed, so did the techniques of job analysis and aptitude measurement. The positive connotation of merit assumed a more definite shape: the measured capacity to perform a specified kind of work well, in fact better than anyone else who was available. But obviously merit has always had a lot of other considerations to compete with. It has never been pure in practice, or even in law. And maybe it should not be, even if we had the knowledge and skill to make it pure. Should a public job be used as a reward (as in veterans' preference)? or as a means of providing income to the needy? or as a device to provide broader representation of various sectors of the society in government? or for other purposes unconnected with the efficiency and effectiveness of getting the work done?

Beyond the Protestant Ethic there were a number of other contributors to the unusual character of American ideals of public service merit. Among these, some of the principal ones were:

individualism—each individual measured on his or her own "merits" in competition with everyone else;

egalitarianism—an open service with equal treatment for all (though within unstated limits) regardless of family, race, religion, social status, formal education, political affiliation;

scientism—faith that there is a correct solution to every personnel question that can be discovered objectively and scientifically; a best person for each job, a correct placement for each person, an accurate classification for each position, a correct wage for each class, and so on;

separatism—resting on the double foundation of nonpolitical merit and scientism, personnel work removed from the rest of government and conducted disinterestedly, scientifically, and independently;

unilateralism—government as sovereign, and its decisions, when reached through proper procedures, final.

The Protestant Ethic with respect to work carries no such compelling authority in our society as it once did, particularly among youth and the disadvantaged. The phenomena described in the three chapters just preceding—professionalism, career systems, and collective bargaining—have all challenged the Protestant Ethic and the other parents of merit principles. Some of the elements long considered extrinsic to merit have become part of the "main course": e.g., transcripts of educational achievement, professional ascription, membership in appropriate organizations, evidences of political or programmatic sympathy with the public hiring agency, political loyalty, personal "suitability." In fields of employee shortage, there is little competition at entrance or in advancement until one reaches the upper grades. Career systems and labor organizations alike seek to protect their members from the competition of outsiders and also tend to reduce competition among their members on the basis of "merit," substituting the less controversial criterion of seniority. Much of the public service is now career oriented; and this means, by and large, that large sectors of it are substantially closed rather than open services. While the scientific drive is on the ascendancy in most fields of knowledge, it seems in personnel administration to be giving ground: to the professions, to the universities, and to collective bargaining. Labor organizations are dislodging civil service commissions from their traditional—and often still cherished—posture of independence; and they are thus driving them into the arms of management. The concept of unilaterialism is directly challenged by both collective bargaining and professionalism, each of which demands increasing influence of employees and their organizations upon governmental decisions.

It is interesting that over many decades the development of civil service, the career systems, the professions, and organized labor had a common enemy: politics and patronage. Perhaps this is why, for the most part, they were accommodating and mutually supportive.[1] But in the places, and to the extent, that the common enemy has been beaten back, it has abandoned the battleground to the former allies, who must contest with each other. One thing seems clear: that the principles of merit and the practices whereby they were given substance are changing and must change a good deal more to remain viable in our society. We can of course continue to use the word, and perhaps we should. But let us not deceive ourselves as to its changing meaning concerning: the determining of merit qualifications; the relations of these to jobs, decisions, and performance in government; the locus of control over job definition and applicant evaluation. We can still have merit systems, but they are not the same as those we inherited from the past and still teach (or delude ourselves) about.

Merit, Equity, and Affirmative Action

The principles of merit in public employment have recently been and are now being most severely challenged by the

1. The same common enemy may also explain the mutually supportive attitudes over the years between the veterans' organizations and civil service, even though, as one student put it, veterans' preference is "essentially the negation of merit." (John F. Miller, "Veteran Preference in the Public Service," *Problems of the American Public Service*, Commission of Inquiry on Public Service Personnel, New York, McGraw-Hill, 1935, p. 309.) But both the merit proponents and veterans opposed patronage.

efforts to enhance the employment opportunities in governments and elsewhere of the alleged victims of present and
past discrimination, minorities (mainly blacks and Hispanics) and women in general.[2] Federal action to eliminate
racial discrimination began as early as 1941 when President
Roosevelt issued an executive order (#8802) forbidding
racial discrimination by defense contractors. Subsequently, in
almost every administration, legal steps to eliminate discrimination on grounds of race or sex or both were taken and
extended—by executive orders, regulations, and statutes.
Requirements for equal employment opportunity now extend to virtually every employing organization of any size in
the United States: the federal government itself; all state and
local governments which receive any grants from the federal
government, including revenue sharing—which means virtually all of them; and all other employers under the Civil
Rights Act of 1964. During the same period, 1941–1981,
there were an accelerating number of court cases, many in
the Supreme Court; most of them ordered greater guarantees
of equal treatment for women and for minorities in employment as well as in education, social services, and other fields
of activity.

There is insufficient space in this book or in any single
book to elucidate the sources of our current problems vis-à-
vis equal employment opportunity. One may say, quite super-
ficially, that they are not primarily due to the behavior of the
current generation. The problem of the blacks is a product
of more than three centuries of slavery, subjugation, depriva-
tion, and segregation. The problem of women is a product of
many centuries of subordination and a cultural division of
labor which consigned most of them to the home and to the

2. I have not included in this discussion certain other categories of
employees, including the physically handicapped, who offer somewhat
different and special problems.

bearing and raising of children. We are in the midst of a cultural revolution involving, on the one hand, blacks and other minority groups and, on the other, women who are in fact a majority and whose problems are quite different. Yet the movements for equal political and civil rights of blacks and of women during the past century have been very roughly coterminous and, in some ways, mutually supportive. Both converged in the third quarter of the twentieth century to create large problems for American society, not least in the administration of public personnel.

There can be no doubt that there are wide statistical disparities in the employment of white males as compared with females and with blacks, Hispanics, and other minorities. In this regard, the record of the federal government is probably better than those of state and local governments and private businesses. But there is not much basis for bragging by any of them. Even where the numbers of female and minority employees are relatively high, their grades and levels of responsibility are, on average, much below those of white males. Pay levels of minority and female employees average far lower than those of white males, and there is evidence of widespread violation of the old and venerated standard of equal pay for equal (or comparable) work—again, in favor of white males. I harbor no doubts that there is still a good deal of discrimination in employment practices against minorities and women in many places and among many organizations, public and private. And I am optimistic enough to believe that the prejudices that give rise to such discrimination are declining. But the main problems are historic in origin and arose from circumstances before the current stage of employment. Rather few blacks and other minorities have been educated to the levels and in the professional fields demanded by governments. And those that have are likely to seek employment outside of public bureaucracies. Women, whose levels of educational achievement may soon surpass those of men, have concentrated on clerical and secretarial skills or on professions only midway in the occupational pecking order—school teaching, nursing, librarianship, social work. As they turn—and they are turning—towards fields of law, business, medicine, engineering, and sciences, the situation will change. But this change will be incremental; it will take many years of changing of perspectives, not only by the women themselves, but also by their husbands, their children, and indeed by society. We are probably demanding of equal employment opportunity programs more than they can deliver. But certainly we should.

It is ironic that problems of public employment should grow out of a collision between actions taken to assure equal employment opportunity (EEO) and merit principles, themselves nurtured by the ideal of equal opportunity, an open public service, and equal treatment for all. Yet, once the issues had surfaced, it became apparent that EEO to become effective might tear at the practice of public personnel administration and at the fabric of merit principles. Could employment opportunities be considered equal when one or more groups of competitors were severely handicapped by deficiencies in education, experience, family background, even language? Could they be considered equal when those same groups of potential competitors were not even advised of their opportunities? Could they be equal when entrance and advancement depended upon examinations which one was not prepared to pass and credentials for which one had little chance to qualify?

It soon became evident that passive programs of equal employment opportunity would not rapidly enhance the opportunities for the minorities or for women. So was born affirmative action, consisting of programs intended positively to motivate and help minority groups and women to seek and gain employment and advancement in public jobs. Affirmative action could be, and was, enthusiastically endorsed by some civil service executives who interpreted it as publicizing job openings and examinations, and eliminating unrealistic job requirements and invalid selection instruments.[3] Merit system purists generally endorsed equal employment opportunity and affirmative action as long as they did not damage or endanger merit system standards. But they generally opposed modification of those standards for social purposes—i.e., purposes other than getting the public job done.[4]

There are a number of actions that may be taken to encourage the employment and advancement of minority personnel and of women, which have been tried in different jurisdictions. They include:

broadening the recruitment base; positive recruitment of candidates among minority and women groups; relaxing or eliminating artificial or unnecessary qualification and credential requirements;

validating and revising examinations so that they test only the knowledges and skills actually needed for the jobs;

restructuring jobs and qualifications so that those with minimal qualifications can be employed and can advance;

providing and supporting in-service as well as outside training to make it possible that those with minimal skills may qualify themselves for promotion;

planning progressive assignments;

relaxing lateral entry restrictions, especially for women;

modifying or, hopefully, eliminating veterans' preference;

reducing the influence of seniority on promotions and retention;

providing more flexible time schedules for women with family responsibilities, such as flexitime and part-time work;

3. See for example Bernard Rosen, then Executive Director, U.S. Civil Service Commission, "Affirmative Action Produces Equal Employment Opportunity for All," *Public Administration Review*, May–June 1974, pp. 237–39.

4. See for example O. Glenn Stahl, *Public Personnel Administration* (7th Ed.), (New York, Harper & Row, 1976), pp. 1, 120–21, 159–60, 166–67.

reviewing and standardizing salary scales in accord with difficulty
   and responsibility of the work, regardless of who is performing
   it;
providing leadership of equal employment opportunity programs within agencies, and unbiased channels of appeal for
   alleged abuses;
establishing goals and schedules for employment of minority and
   female personnel;
keeping complete records on all candidates, appointments, promotions and other employment actions and of the methods
   followed in connection with each.

Most of the above kinds of action have been used in some
or many public jurisdictions as well as in private businesses,
and there is little question as to their propriety. But by and
large they have not been conspicuously effective in increasing and elevating the employment of female and minority
personnel. More aggressive proponents of affirmative action
have urged, and in many places used, other tools, some of
which directly challenge long-established principles of merit.
They include:

waiving examinations for original appointments, or substituting
   qualifying (pass-fail) tests for competitive examinations;
hiring underqualified people for part-time or temporary work;
providing them with education and training while on the job;
giving them civil service status without examination; employing
   them as professionals after their training;
redesigning work levels and jobs to permit unqualified persons
   to be appointed and learn on the job so that they may gain civil
   service status;
establishing and enforcing quotas for minority employees and
   women;
selective certification for appointment on the basis of race or sex;
lowering standards and qualifications for appointments below a
   minimum adequate for job performance;

discriminating in the certification, hiring, and promoting of personnel in favor of women and minorities;

exclusion of nonminority males from competition or consideration for appointment or promotion for certain kinds of jobs.

Most of the kinds of actions listed in the first and second categories above are endorsed, sometimes reluctantly, by practitioners and adherents of merit systems, whether or not in the civil service. Most of those in the third list they vehemently oppose as violative of merit principles. Some of these are obviously discriminatory against males other than minority and, in effect, constitute reverse discrimination. They raise two related issues of profound importance in current American society.

1. Should we use our practices in public employment to help correct inequities in our society, even if they detract from efficiency and effectiveness in the delivery of public services?
2. Should we use our current employment practices to correct inequities we have inherited from the past and for which the current generations are minimally responsible, or should we simply assure equity in our personnel transactions for the present and future?

Merit system purists tend to respond to both questions in the negative, feeling that actions to correct social ills will undermine the principles of merit. On the other hand some representatives of minority and feminist groups have been militant in advocating personnel measures to correct past abuses, often called compensatory employment, even when such actions seem to constitute reverse discrimination against most white males. Meanwhile, the judicial branch has been increasingly involved in the very marrow of personnel work in both the public and private sectors through cases brought by alleged victims of discrimination or reverse discrimination. These have involved: the relevance of qualification requirements and credentials to specific jobs; the relevance and validity of examinations; the analysis and classifications of positions; the criteria used in promotions; the use of quotas in recruitment and selection; and many others. A most important case was one recently brought by members of minority groups against the federal Office of Personnel Management on the grounds that its Professional and Administrative Career Examination (PACE) discriminated against blacks and Hispanics and included questions which had no bearing on the jobs the candidates would be expected to perform. The PACE examination was the latest version of a series of general tests begun almost fifty years ago to screen college graduates for junior posts in a great variety of fields (118 different classes of positions) as a beginning of a government career. The case was settled out of court when the government, apparently doubtful that it could win, agreed to replace the test with separate tests for each of the 118 classes of positions.[5]

The drive toward fair employment practices, including the frequent involvement of the courts, has not been without benefit for the public service and its management. It has forced greater attention to the analysis of jobs and to the drafting of qualification requirements that are more realistic, forced greater efforts to validate tests, and helped create more defensible criteria for promotions. It has undoubtedly reduced overt discrimination, although I doubt that it has eliminated it; and it has undoubtedly given rise in some places to reverse discrimination. The public services are probably more representative, at least in the passive sense, but progress has been slow and is likely to be slower as public employment ceases to grow.

Not least among the costs of affirmative action has been the increasing involvement of the courts and of litigation. Public managers generally and personnel administrators particularly must now increasingly make their decisions on the basis not

5. *New York Times*, Jan. 10, 1981, p. 16.

of managerial and public interest considerations but of how they will look to a judge who, in most instances, has never had managerial responsibilities.

Administrative Morality

During this period when the traditional principles of merit are being challenged, similar forces are undermining the old articles of faith through which administration and democracy were reconciled. The ideological crutch which segregated policy and politics from administration can today hardly satisfy any but the blind or those who willfully close their eyes. The idea of objective responsibility is increasingly threatened by both professionalization and unionization, with their narrow objectives and their focus upon the welfare and advancement of their members. At the same time, the idea of representative bureaucracy has acquired a meaning which is not altogether reassuring to the general public interest. Most of the professions are well represented in their appropriate enclaves, as are most of those growing categories of employees who join in collective organizations. Even the poor may lay some claim to representation in the community councils, though its effectiveness is at least questionable. But who represents that majority of citizens who are not in any of these groups?

The problems introduced in the opening chapter of this study appear not to have been resolved through the developments described in the later chapters. On the contrary, they have been aggravated. The knowledge explosion and the tremendous growth of higher education have greatly enhanced the technical and cognitive capacities of the public service to perform its tasks. At the same time, may they not have weakened its concern for, and competence in, reaching social decisions responsibly with the full polity in view?

This is essentially a moral question; indeed it is *the* moral question of the public service in American democracy.

Among the larger units of American government, the older and more overt violations of individual honesty and trust have been minimized. In terms of the billions of dollars involved in governmental transactions every day, the amount of theft, fraud, bribery, and even expense account padding are today comparatively small. Few sectors of American society are more carefully policed in these regards than the administrative arms of its larger governments.

The harder and infinitely more important issue of administrative morality today attends the reaching of decisions on questions of public policy which involve competitions in loyalty and perspective between broad goals of the polity (the phantom public interest) and the narrower goals of a group, bureau, clientele, or union. Chester I. Barnard defined administrative responsibility as primarily a moral question or, more specifically, as the resolution of competing and conflicting codes—legal, technical, personal, professional, and organizational—in the reaching of individual decisions.[6] Barnard wrote primarily of business administration; students of government would add a less definable but nevertheless all-important code—the public benefit.

The danger is that developments in the public service may be subtly, gradually, but profoundly moving the weight toward the partial, the corporate, the professional perspective and away from that of the general interest. In this connection a number of developments noted earlier may be reviewed:

the tendency of "elite" professions to dominate the governance of bureaus and other public agencies;

the dominance in matters of recruitment, selection, and advancement of professional groups, both in and outside government, and the declining influence of general government agencies;

the deepening of professional specializations;

6. In *The Functions of the Executive* (Cambridge, Harvard University Press, 1948), Chapter XVII.

the development of self-governing professional career systems within public agencies;

the corporatism of organized public employees, especially those in professional and subprofessional fields.

The multifarious systems of American government include a variety of built-in institutional and procedural devices to protect against such narrowly based, functionally parochial decisions. Most familiar are the divisions and sharing of functions and powers of government among different levels and units; the division and sharing of powers among executive, legislative, and judicial branches; the various devices of executive co-ordination and control, including particularly the executive budget; and appointive political leadership. Clearly, however, occupational groups can successfully overpass most of these hurdles, and in some cases indeed use them to their own power advantage. The division of official and legitimate power among many satrapies (units of government, executive bureaus, legislative committees) strengthens the influence of the unified occupational group which has a common perspective and objective.

As Paul H. Appleby demonstrated in his book *Morality and Administration in Democratic Government*,[7] the traditional and popularized protections against immorality in public administration—checks and balances, decentralization, federalism, and others—are a good deal less than effective. In fact their protective value is probably, on balance, negative. Appleby relied instead on two other (and in considerable degree antipodal) institutional mechanisms to assure morality in the public service. One is found in the workings of an open system of politics and administration wherein administrative behavior and decisions are exposed or may be exposed and must ultimately be judged against their potential influence in the ballot box. Any effort to remove an area of

7. Baton Rouge, Louisiana State University Press, 1952.

governmental activity from general political responsibility—
to "protect" it from politics is, per se, a threat to administrative morality, since it encourages the administrator to
approach his problems narrowly, to minimize or neglect or
ignore the general interest. Appleby wrote long before there
was any general freedom of information law on the books,
but there is little doubt that he would have been an ardent
supporter of the aims of such legislation.

The second protective mechanism, according to Appleby,
is hierarchy within administration which, if effective, forces
important decisions to higher levels of determination or at
least higher levels of review where perspectives are necessarily
broader, less technical and expert, more political. Unlike
some other writers on administration of his time, Appleby
minimized the significance of hierarchy as a basis of authority.
He liked to quote Chester Barnard to the effect that
"experienced and effective administrators prefer not to use
authority."[8] Hierarchy, on the other hand, is a means to
broaden the perspective for, and the responsibility of,
decision.

The establishment of professional enclaves within public
agencies is of course a very direct threat to both of Appleby's
protective mechanisms: open politics and responsible hierarchy. By removing itself as far as possible from the normal
channels of political complaint, debate, and appeal, a professionally dominated agency denies the general public the
opportunity for democratic direction and decision. By closing
the elite of the hierarchy to all but professionals, it denies
assurance of broadly based and disinterested judgment on
problems.

In fact, Appleby perceived as dangerous to democracy
many of the developments noted in earlier chapters of this
volume. He felt, even more vigorously than some of his

8. Ibid. p. 205.

contemporaries, the danger of experts being "on top rather than on tap." "Perhaps there is no single problem in public administration of moment equal to the reconciliation of the increasing dependence upon experts with an enduring democratic reality."[9] He feared that functional specialization within agencies would result in "relative inattention to the large public" and pointed particularly to one form of this: "preoccupation with subject-matter expertise, as with economics, law, medicine, biology, physics, etc."—fields that represent all the professions.[10] Finally, he feared the effects of what I have called career systems of personnel administration —overreliance upon promotions from within, closing the door to outside recruitment, overemphasis upon security and seniority. Were Appleby writing today, his alarums would no doubt be shriller because some of the recent developments were only on the horizon at the time when he wrote of administrative morality. Professional (as against civil service) control of personnel is now much more evident; political appointees, the broadly based generalists upon whom he relied so heavily and of whom he was one, are increasingly professionalized and specialized themselves; the knowledge explosion has much more closely linked government professionals with their subject-matter counterparts in the universities and has given a far stronger scientific-expertise flavor to public administration.

Had Appleby lived through the Watergate episode, his views would probably have been somewhat different and probably less sanguine. Watergate confirmed his faith in open politics; in fact, the greater part of the scandals resulted from the deliberate closing of political channels and the cover-up of information. But his faith in hierarchy and in political leadership would surely have been shaken. What

9. Ibid. p. 145.
10. Ibid. p. 145.

good is hierarchy when many of those at the top have warped or narrow views of the public interest and are themselves liars and criminals?

In his writings about administrative morality, Paul Appleby addressed himself principally to the institutional arrangements which tended to encourage or to endanger moral behavior. He did not dwell upon the ethical problems of individual public servants or groups thereof. In 1965, this lacuna was eloquently corrected by Stephen K. Bailey in a memorial essay to Appleby.[11] Bailey, building upon precepts drawn from Appleby's writings, teachings, and actions, synthesized the essentials of moral behavior in public service in two categories: moral qualities and mental attitudes. The essential moral qualities are three: optimism, courage, and fairness tempered by charity. The words in all three cases are inadequate to the intended meaning. Optimism is the confidence and capacity to deal with ambiguous situations constructively and purposively. Courage is the ability to decide and act in the face of difficulties for which withdrawal would be an easier response, and to abide by principle even in unpopular causes. Fairness tempered by charity is demanded by the standards of justice and the necessity that value-laden decisions be governed by the public interest.

The "mental attitudes" which Bailey identifies as requisites of personal ethics in the public service are also three in number. All are cognitive in nature, based upon knowledge and understanding and therefore learnable and teachable. They consist of recognition of 1. the moral ambiguity of all persons and of all public policies; 2. the contextual forces which condition moral priorities in the public service; and 3. the paradoxes of procedures. Under the first of these, Bailey stresses the ambivalence of most public decisions as

---

11. "Ethics and the Public Service," in Roscoe C. Martin (ed.), *Public Administration and Democracy: Essays in Honor of Paul H. Appleby* (Syracuse, Syracuse University Press, 1965).

between personal and private interests and the public interest, and as a corollary, the morally ambivalent effect of public policies. Seldom, if ever, can a policy be either totally right or totally wrong. In his reference to the awareness of context, Bailey emphasizes the shifting of value priorities, the necessity of flexibility, and the increasing difficulty and complexity of value-choices as one rises in the hierarchy. In his reference to procedures, Bailey again stresses flexibility; the use of laws, rules, and procedures to promote fairness and openness; and notes the abuse of laws, rules, and procedures to prevent action and obscure the public interest.

The Barnard-Appleby-Bailey construct of responsibility and morality in public decision-making provides a sound base for a philosophy of a public service which is both consistent with and supportive of democracy. The construct contains certain ingredients which, though fairly obvious, are not universally accepted or even recognized. One is that there is a high ethical content in most significant public decisions; public problems seldom succumb simply to factual analysis. A second is that the standards of ethical behavior that are applicable and sufficient to a private citizen in his private social relationships are not in themselves adequate for the public decisions of an administrator. The same limitation applies to professional codes of ethics in their applicability to decisions by professionals in the public service. The public character of governmental decisions adds complicating dimensions to moral behavior. A third is that public decision problems are seldom black or white in relation to their ethical content and consequences. This is another way of saying that they are difficult and that the "best" solution is seldom without its costs. Finally—and least understood— is the proposition that politics and administrative organization are themselves the best protectors of administrative morality, provided they are open and public.

But if we can accept the Barnard-Appleby-Bailey construct as a philosophic base, how can it be made operational among

administrators? Must each one learn it for himself by succes-
sive burnings of his fingers—as, for the most part, Barnard
and Appleby and Bailey must have done? Not many administrators are as perceptive and sensitive as these three, and one
doubts that such an experiential process would be very
effective, even in the very long range. Further, it is clear that
some of the central tenets of this view of public morality run
directly counter to the doctrine of a number of professions
which are important sources of public administrators—
probably the majority of them. Most professions are at best
ambivalent, at worst downright hostile, toward government
in general and politics in particular. Most seek to shield
themselves from politics, and this of course means that they
oppose *open* politics. Most oppose the incursion of nonprofessionals into their professional decision-making territory.
Most of those which have to do primarily with things rather
than people are impatient with ambiguities, with compromise, with administrative procedure. Those professions
which are applied sciences or which emulate or aspire to be
sciences—and this includes the majority of them—emphasize
values and processes consistent with the search for knowledge
and truth. The exigencies of public problems, imperfectly
defined and demanding actions on the basis of partial and
often questionable information, are seldom consonant with
such values and processes. The recent thrust of many of the
professions is not very promising for the development of the
kind of administrative morality envisaged by Barnard,
Appleby, and Bailey.

Democracy and Education

The winds of change, however, bear other straws, straws
which promise new and more meaningful definitions of
"merit" and also a broader and deeper understanding of
administrative responsibility. One of these straws is simply
the urgency of public problems. The underdeveloped popu-

lations of the world are impatient, as are our own minorities, our own impoverished, our own urban populations. Action will not wait for the completion of data-gathering and analysis or for the negotiation of boundaries between occupational monopolies. A second straw is a product of the knowledge explosion itself, which among other things has taught the interconnection of social conditions and the obstinacy of any social problem to respond to a specific, functionally defined solution. The educators by themselves are unable to cope with the problem of education, because it goes far beyond teaching. The doctors and the health officers are confronted with the same situation in the area of health, as are the police in that of crime, the transportation engineers in transportation, the welfare workers in poverty, and all of these in racial discrimination and hostility. Each profession is learning the hard way of its own inadequacies and its underlying dependence upon the methods and understandings of other disciplines. The interdisciplinary and interprofessional approach is no longer a mere academic curio, an interesting but dilettantish experiment. In today's world it is an absolute necessity, for no discipline, no profession, can handle even its own problems by itself. This lesson was learned a good many years ago by the natural sciences and the "natural" professions. It is coming later and harder in the social fields, particularly economics; but its ultimate acceptance is inevitable. The interconnection of social problems and the interdependence of disciplines in dealing with them are two sides of the same coin.

Another product of the knowledge explosion has been a growing faith of the society and particularly of its leaders in the value of research to enable us more effectively to deal with our problems. This growth also started in the physical sciences and is least questioned there. It has recently spread rapidly in the life and medical sciences. It is beginning to develop in the social sciences. It is interesting, paradoxical, and indeed tragic that government has so tremendously stimulated and supported the natural sciences while giving the back of its hand to those fields of social knowledge upon which government and the society itself most immediately depend. Our hardest problems are human problems that can respond only to human remedies. We are beginning to learn how to analyze these problems and to devise means of coping with them. Social policies must be focused on values, tempered by sympathy, grounded in knowledge.

The higher officials in the public service are products of the colleges and universities, and principally their professional departments and schools. This will be increasingly, even mayhap exclusively, true in the future. These persons will have a growing influence in the determination of public policy. Ultimately the possibilities of a truly democratic public service will depend upon 1. the mobility whereby intelligent individuals from all walks of life may progress to and through higher education and 2. the kind of orientation and education they receive in the universities. On the first point there is evidence of progress, though there is a long way to go. On the second, in spite of centripetal, problem-oriented pressures described earlier, there remains a high degree of specialization in particular fields accompanied by a declining exposure to, and interest in, broader social areas, including the context within which each specialization operates.

In the future, merit will increasingly be measured by professionals against criteria established by the professions and by the universities which spawn them. It will depend in part upon technical and cognitive qualifications in the fields of specialization. The danger is that these will be too large a part of the criteria. Truly meritorious performance in public administration will depend at least equally upon the values, the objectives, and the moral standards which the administrator brings to his decisions, and upon his ability to weigh the relevant premises judiciously in his approach to the problems at hand. His code can hardly be as simple as the

Ten Commandments, the Boy Scout Code, or the code of ethics of any of the professions; his decisions usually will require some kind of interpretation of *public and public interest*—explicit, implicit, even unconscious.

Such decisions are difficult, complex, and soul-testing, for the qualities they demand search the depths of both mind and spirit. As Bailey wrote, "Virtue without understanding can be quite as disastrous as understanding without virtue."[12] Understanding entails a degree of knowledge, a sense of relationships among phenomena, an appreciation of both social and private values. Most of the ingredients of understanding can be learned, and many of them can be taught. They go well beyond the mastery of scientific method, of substantive knowledge, of professional technique. They go beyond the boundaries of the typical profession or the curriculum of the standard professional training course. Yet understanding in this sense must become a major ingredient of public service merit in the future. This will require a degree of modesty and even humility on the part of individual professionals (and professors) about their fields; a curiosity about, and accommodation toward, other fields of study and vocation; a sense of the society and the polity, and of the relationships between them and the field of occupational concentration.

Governmental agencies have for the most part accepted professional and academic definitions and measurements of merit as applied to specific academic and occupational fields. Most of them have, however, minimized the broader understanding discussed in the preceding paragraph as an element in appointment or advancement. The more difficult, less measurable, elements of morality in public decision-making have been almost completely ignored in discussions of merit principles, although they may well be the most important criteria of all.

12. Ibid. p. 285.

As in our culture in the past and in a good many other civilizations, the nature and quality of the public service depend principally upon the system of education. Almost all of our future public administrators will be college graduates, and within two or three decades a majority of them will probably have graduate degrees. Rising proportions of public administrators are returning to graduate schools for refresher courses, mid-career training, and higher degrees. These trends suggest that university faculties will have growing responsibility for preparing and for developing public servants both in their technical specialities and in the broader social fields with which their professions interact.

The universities offer the best means of making the professions safe for democracy. At least one may hope.

Name Index

Name Index

Subject Index

Subject Index

CPSIA information can be obtained
at www.ICGtesting.com
Printed in the USA
FFOW04n1936220117
31586FF